Confidence, Communication And You

The survival guide to the modern world

MAWGEN SCHOEMAN

WWW.NLPMINDSOLUTIONS.COM

CONTENTS

Part 1 – How to get what you want

Part 2 – Unstoppable confidence

Part 3 – Effective communication

ACKNOWLEDGEMENTS

Our thanks first go to Sean McPheat's for the amazing work put together in the creation of the 6 module e-courses and the inspiration for putting this book together. I would also like to thank every person who is involved in the business of coaching and NLP for carrying and evolving the personal development industry.

ABOUT THIS BOOK

The best way to approach this book is to see it as three separate workshops that completes a big picture and you are welcome to do the three parts in any order. lets look at the sections:

Part 1 - Unstoppable Confidence

Part 1 consists of 6 chapters that is designed to assist you in getting self-confidence. Each of the chapters includes a number of exercises and assignments that will teach you all you need to know in order to build your confidence.

"Unstoppable Confidence" will enable you to smash through those barriers and limited beliefs that you have about yourself and move forward with your life. Without confidence you will never be able to lead the life that you want. Confident people are successful people. They stick out a mile don't they? Many people in life have the same amount of skills but what holds them back is their lack of self-belief.

Part 2 - How To Get What You Want In Life

Part 2 consists of 6 chapters that is designed to provide you with the direction, purpose and drive that they are looking for.

Each of the chapters includes a number of exercises and assignments that will walk you through the process of first working out what you want from your life and then, how you are going to get it. The course will enable you to stop drifting along in life – instead you will discover what your life is all about and how you can go about to improve it. You only live once so you'd better make the most of the time whilst you are here!

"How to get what you want" will be your very own life map of where you are now to where you want to get to. You will soon rediscover those lost ambitions, those dreams that had fallen by the wayside.

Part 3 - Effective Communication Skills

Part 3 consist of 6 chapters that is designed to improve your communications skills enabling you to express yourself more clearly and to talk with confidence and assurance. Each of the chapters includes a number of exercises and assignments that will teach you all you need to know so that you can communicate more effectively with all of the people who you come in contact with.

With "Effective Communication Skills" you will now be able to know what effective communications are all about, how the great communicators do it and all there is to know about non-verbal communication techniques which make up to 93% of all communications! Communication is so vital to everything that anyone does because we are usually required to seek solutions, information and help from others.

It is without doubt the most important skill that anyone can improve and let me tell you that the results of doing so can be outstanding. The results can improve your relationships with clients and colleagues, loved ones and associates – you name it!

Everyone can communicate in one shape or form. But haven't you seen those people whose communication and interpersonal skills just seem to be on another level? They seem to have everyone doing whatever they say, the person is liked and respected by all, they can talk to strangers and build up rapport effortlessly!

That's the difference between communicating and communicating effectively. Communication goes far beyond the actual words that you say. More importantly it's how you say it and the way that you act while you're saying it.

So how about we get started.

Part 1

How to Get What You Want

If you think you can, you
can.

Introduction

When asked how he got all he wanted, Texas multi-millionaire H. L. Hunt said, "You have to make up your mind, what you want. You have to make up your mind, what you are prepared to give up getting it. You have to set your priorities, and then go about your job." Coming from someone who started with running cotton plantations and ended up making a fortune in oil business, these words are something to be seriously taken note off.

"How to Get What you Want" are 6 parts that is designed to provide you with the direction, purpose and drive that you are looking for.

Each of the 6 includes a number of exercises and assignments that will walk you through the process of first working out what you want from your life and then, how you are going to get it.

It will enable you to stop drifting along in life – instead you will discover what your life is all about and how you can go about to improve it.

"How to Get What you Want" will be your very own life map of where you are now to where you want to reach. You will soon rediscover those lost ambitions, those dreams that had fallen by the wayside.

This is the time to start afresh.

So start right now!

1-1

Discover What Your Life is Really About

Life is so short that you cannot wait for your wishes to be fulfilled. Neither is it generous enough to you to take everything for granted. However, it is possible to design your life in a way you can go out and grab whatever you want.

Welcome to "How to Get What You Want!"

First of all, you need to have a clear picture of where you are at right now. Then realize what it is that you truly want from life. Develop a clear understanding of what you need and what you do not. The next 6 modules will help you comprehend your wants, and find the ways to make sure that you are going to fulfill them all.

Everyone is evaluated on the basis of his or her successes. However, success does not mean the same thing to everyone. In the first session, you will have a close look at what success actually means to you and then we will discuss what the purpose of your life is.

This session is the underpinning on which others are based. Moreover, it deals with the things that set the foundation on what your life is based on.

What is Success?

Everyone wants to be a success in his or her life. People consider material success as the key to more money, happiness, fulfillment and rewards. Regardless of how differently people perceive it, everyone wants it.

Different people define success differently. And they tend to change their definition with changing times and circumstances as well. For some people, conventional success is more important and it seldom goes beyond money, cars or big homes.

You must have your own definition for success. However, you don't have to be dogmatic about this. You can change your definition of success and put it closer to reality. Before that you need to comprehend what success actually means to you.

Write your definition of what success is in the space below or on a piece of paper.

Do not carry on reading this until you have done so.

It may take a good amount of time to sort out your priorities when you define what success means. Don't cheat yourself!

Who is successful?

Bob is a 32-year old store assistant. His wife Anne is 30 years old and works in the administrative section at a small local firm. They live in their small suburban cottage with two children. Bob leaves his shop at 6 pm every evening and is greeted by his wife at the door with a kiss and a hug.

Bob finds time to play games with his children and every night reads them a story. Despite financial constraints the family goes on a vacation every year. They spend a lot of time together.

Another case.

Mary Jane is a 28-year old single woman. Her job as a Financial Analyst enables her to maintain a posh apartment in the City and own a Lexus. She could afford a holiday anywhere in the world, though she rarely goes out of the City if it's not on an official trip.

Her hectic workload seldom allows Mary Jane to reach home before 7 pm or to go out for a party. Lack of socialization often gives her a feeling of loneliness, though she believes that the money makes up for it. She is ready to put aside her personal feelings for a career that gives her enough money and social status.

Okay, the question now is **who do you think is successful of the two – Bob or Mary Jane?**

If you are a teenager you would have selected Jane without doubt. She maintains a great lifestyle, has a good job and plenty of money.

If you are older and yearn for contentment in life, then you would probably select Bob, the happier one with a contented and fulfilled life.

Compare your selection with the definition you have written in the box above. You can see that your selection and your definition have a lot in common.

A person defines success on the basis of a number of factors. And you are no exception.

Your definition of success is formed by:

- Your upbringing
  Everyone perceives things on the basis of the values he or she has learned in the childhood.

- Your beliefs
  Beliefs, deep-rooted in your mind, affect the way you perceive things.

- Trait
  A particular characteristic that distinguishes you or that is genetically determined may influence the way you perceive things.
- Your attitude
  Everyone has an opinion or general feeling about everything.
- Your peers
  You family, friends, colleagues or whoever you maintain a constant contact with can influence the way you perceive things.
- Society
  It is an important factor that has more influence than many of the rest.
- Every experience that you have in life
  Small or big, each and every experience in your life influences the way you perceive things.

All the factors mentioned above, more or less, contribute to what success means to you.

There is a myth that states that people are born winners or born losers.

Nothing could be further from the truth. Nobody is born just to win or lose. The way you live your life makes you a winner or loser.

As Benjamin Disraeli puts it, "The secret of success is constancy to purpose." Using some techniques and methods and improving your attitude, behavior and personality can lead you to destination called success.

More often than not, you are responsible for what you get from life.

Even a single sensible timely step can change the entire scenario. You need to sense what the situation demands and act accordingly. Nothing is worse than looking back after some years and saying "I wish I had done this."

Know where you are going in life

Setting goals is something everybody does regularly. However, few find it in them to go through the plans they set. You need to know where you are going and constantly check and make sure that you are moving in the proper direction.

Creating a vision and a mission statement of what you want out of life will provide you with some direction and momentum to move forward. It can act as a catalyst in accomplishing your task.

What is your life all about?

Different people look at life in entirely different ways. While some people let things happen to them, others go out and make things happen. It's very important to have an understanding of which group you belong to.

If you are driven by a compelling vision, you have a greater chance to feel good about yourself.

If you have a true mission, you have a better chance to know where you are going in your life.

When you feel you are in control of your life and events, you will naturally feel more confident and motivated to achieve more.

Ask yourself the following question:

What do you really want to get out of life?

A clear vision and a well-defined mission will help you realize the real purpose of your life. Both your vision and mission should express your purpose for existence.

Following is a series of questions for you to ask yourself in order to do some soul searching and to give yourself some insights into what you are all about and why you are here:

- "When I grow up, I want to be a pilot." As a child, what did you dream of becoming?
- Which three people do you think have influenced your life the most and why?
- If you could choose your career and get paid whatever you wanted, what would you opt for?

- What are your top three achievements in life so far? What was so special about them?
- Doing what makes you the happiest in life?
- Who are the three people who you admire the most? What are their characteristics and qualities you admire so much?
- Have you ever helped someone less fortunate than you? If yes, what did you do? If no, why not?
- List out your greatest strengths?
- What steps should you take in life to maximize your strengths?
- What is that one thing for which you would be willing to put everything on the block for? Why?
- Imagine that all the time you spent till now comes back to you. How would you utilize it now? What would you do with the time this second time round?
- There are sure to be results/ events in your life you are happy about? What are these? Which are the results/ events you are unhappy about?
- Is there a word of advice you have picked up from your life so far that you want to pass on to the world?
- Name one thing you value the most in life?
- What would you really like to do with your life?

Answering the questions given above will give you a clear idea about yourself.

The whole point of getting you to think about those questions was to really get you to think about what you want and wanted for your life.

It would be easier for you, after answering the questions, to realize what you want from life and how you are going to get it. If you have answered all the questions given above, write down your own mission statement right now!

A mission statement is not a 'to do list.' So it is not easy to write one and it shouldn't be something that is rushed.

Take your time, go for a walk, or take a short break. It's better to get away from the routine environment. Remember, your mission in life is far too important to be skimmed over.

A mission statement needs to be honest. Make sure you actually believe in your mission statement. If you don't, it's a lie. Don't cheat yourself.

People who do not have an authentic mission in life tend to just have materialistic goals. The greatest problem with such people is they don't know what fulfillment is. After they have achieved, achieved and achieved, they say to themselves "Is that all there is?"

Elvis Presley, also known as "The King of Rock 'n' Roll," was a giant in the modern entertainment industry. Few people influenced American popular culture like Presley. Wealth, fame, women, success...all the pleasures of life were plentiful in his life.

However, when Presley killed himself by overdosing on a stash of drugs he stocked, he was only 42 years old. Despite all his successes, he followed a self-destructive lifestyle.

Presley was a man who owned what others dreamed about. His success was legendary and his achievements were enviable. However, without a sense of fulfilment, there is no joy.

Success without fulfillment is failure!

Your mission statement says only about what you really want to be in life.

We can go one step ahead to understand how we want our life to look in the end. That broadens our insights even more.

A method of doing that is to write your own obituary. It will give you a comprehensive picture of what all you want to achieve in life and how it should be in the end.

Specially note down the things you will be remembered for even after a long time.

Write your obituary, now.

Okay! That's it for chapter 1.

Hope this session gave you a lot to think and reconsider.

Delve deep into the spheres of your mind, your heart, and let the inner secrets reveal something valuable to your life. Then work out the assignment again.

Good Luck! See you in the next session.

1-2

The Goal Setting Workshop: Mapping Out What You Want in Your Life

Welcome to the second session of How to Get What You Want.

The first session was meant to give you an idea about what success is and the emptiness of success without fulfillment.

Hopefully you have put some things into perspective in your life, right?

So, now you have a clear vision and an honest mission statement for your life. The roadmap to a successful and fulfilled life is within your hands. What's more, you even have your own obituary with you.

After completing those exercises did you find that you would need to start work on some things and to stop certain things as well?

Assignment 1

Before we carry on, please have a quick read over what you put down in the last session. Keeping what you have learned in mind, answer the questions given below:

- What was the one learning point that came out of the exercise more than any other?
- What are you going to start to do?
- What are you going to stop?
- What have you been putting up with in the past that you shouldn't have been?
- What are you going to do instead of this?
- What are you going to move towards in the future?

Anyone can make a new start any time.

Complete the following goal setting workshop to focus on what you want in the future. To accomplish great things, we must learn to dream first.

You need to dream to make them come true. So, throughout the exercise, keep dreaming. Let there be no limits!

OK, here comes the exercise!

Create Your Goals

Certainty and uncertainty are two phases of life. Both contribute immensely to your confidence and lack of confidence.

In order to feel confident you need to have some certainty in your life. You need to be convinced that what you are doing is contributing to an end result.

People often set goals with the intention of achieving them. Many strive for it, but only a few succeed. A wrong step or small mistake could spoil the efforts of a very long time. Then you will start wondering why, despite all your efforts, success evades you. Such feelings might seriously affect your confidence.

We are all goal seeking animals and you are no exception. In fact we set numerous goals a day and strive for them simultaneously in the different areas of our life.

Have you got any goals mapped out for each area of your life?

If not, then read on and complete this exercise.

Goal Creation Exercise:

With regards to the following areas in your life:
- Career
- Relationships
- Fun
- Achievements
- Money
- Possessions

Take 6 pieces of paper for the 6 areas given above. Under each heading, brainstorm for 3 minutes and write down all of the things you would like to achieve in each area.

You don't have to be scared of or worry about the size of your goal. Just get them down and don't think too much about them - Just keep writing!

After you have completed the first part of the exercise you should have 6 pieces of paper full of everything that you would like to achieve for each area.

Next, write down a time limit next to each of the goals. The time limit should be reasonable as well as realistic.

The suggested timescales are:

- Less than 1 year
- 1 – 3 years
- 3 years plus

So, you have got 6 lists of things that you want to achieve in the 6 areas of your life, and the timescale for each.

Next, take your LESS THAN 1 YEAR goals for each area and select the top 2 from each.

So now you have got 12 goals that you can achieve within 1 year.

A strong need or a real motivation is essential to achieve any goal. It is the key. So, before we start to write down an action plan (that's the next chapter) of how to achieve each goal, write down the compelling reasons why achieving each goal is an absolute must for you.

Knowing is as important as doing. You need to check that if your motivations are strong enough to take you to the end.

Unless you have compelling reasons why you MUST make these goals happen, you will not have the motivation to achieve them.

Having goals that are "SHOULDS" will not get you out of bed each day and keep you up late! Moreover too many "SHOULDS" can act as a deterrent. So, you've got to turn your "I SHOULD DO THIS" to "I MUST DO THIS."

Answer the following questions for each of your goals.

What pleasure will it give you?

What will you be able to do with it?

What will you miss if you don't complete it?

Why is it so important to you?

Why is it a MUST rather than a SHOULD?

To recap then!

- Brainstorm what you want in each area of your life
- Put timescales next to each
- Select your less than 1 year goals
- Pick 2 goals from each
- Write down the compelling reasons why achieving each in less than one year is a must

That's it for now.

In the next session we will have a detailed look at your goals and prepare action plans for each!

1-3

Fire The Gun! – How To Take Action

Welcome to chapter three!

First of all, let's have a quick recap of what we have covered so far.

In the first session you had a look at what success means to you and had written out what you would like to be remembered for long after you have gone.

In the second session you made a list of goals you want to achieve and found out the compelling reasons of why you want to achieve them. Also, you had set time limits for each goal to be achieved.

OK, now take the list of goals out, and re-read the reasons. Do they make you feel energized and motivated, and induce a feeling of necessity inside you? Do you feel achieving them is something you can't afford missing?

If they don't, you need to find out better reasons. Or you erred in selecting the particular goal. It does not deserve a place in your list. Scrap the goal altogether!

You will only achieve a goal when it becomes an absolute MUST for you to do so. A goal is nothing but a daydream if you don't have compelling reasons behind it.

It's not the goal but the reasons behind it that make you take action.

Following are some goals you might have included in your list:

Losing some weight

Running your own business

Working harder

Spending more time with your family

Being more assertive

Teaching your child to ride a bicycle

Gaining a better job or promotion

Doing charity work

Owning a new car

Improving your relationship with your boss

Writing a diary

Earning more money

Learning to swim

Controlling your temper

Paying more attention to your clothes

The following is a simple description about setting and achieving a goal.

First of all, you must decide what your GOAL actually is. Then you must define it comprehensively. Next you can lay out the steps by which you intend to reach the goal. And finally you must put a deadline or a time limit to achieve your goal.

And, needless to say, you must also have a genuine reason why you want to achieve the goal.

The goal setting process can be compared with a long distance car journey.

You wouldn't think of planning the journey without knowing where you were going to go and why you want to go there.

You would have mapped out the route, and have an idea of the time it would take to reach your destination

Sounds familiar, doesn't it?

Well, goal setting uses exactly the same method, except in this case, you are the car and the journey is your life.

When it comes to setting your goals, clarity and preciseness are most required qualities. Generalizations and vague ideas won't get you anywhere.

Ask anyone on the street to define their goals in life. You would invariably get responses such as "I want to be rich," "I want to be happy" or "I want to be famous."

Never let yourself be fooled into thinking that these were goals. They are not.

They are just generalizations that are desired by everyone.

A goal needs to be defined in detail. Or a true goal is something you can define in detail. This step comes just after the identification of the goal. If, for example, one of your goals is to buy a new car, you must define the model, the color, the interior, the price and other details.

Always make sure that you can picture it clearly in your mind and try to get away from generalizations.

Be specific and be precise.

GOAL - TO BUY A NEW CAR

Details

MODEL - BMW 3 series sports convertible

COLOUR - Metallic Blue

INTERIOR - Beige Leather

PRICE - £25,450

EXTRAS - Air Conditioning, CD player,

Electric Windows..........

Given above are the primary details. You can go to secondary or tertiary details to exactly know what you want.

Consider the following questions:

What colour are the seats?

What brand is the CD player?

Has it got Electric Windows?

Does it have a sunroof?

Is the sunroof electric?

Has it got alloy wheels?

DO NOT GENERALISE, KNOW EXACTLY WHAT YOU WANT

HOW TO ACHIEVE YOUR GOAL - PLANNING AND ACTION

Now you know what you want to achieve and you have defined it in detail. The next step is to actually plan and map out exactly how you are going to achieve it.

Your desire is not enough to achieve a goal. You need to have the courage, will and an action plan to achieve a goal.

Remember, it is a lot easier to achieve a goal if it is broken down into a series of sub-goals. Each sub-goal, with its own specific deadline, should lead you to the ultimate one. Moreover, when a goal breaks into many sub-goals, you are expected to tackle it sequentially, completing one sub-goal before moving to next.

Consider the following example

You want to lose some weight. Make the goal more specific.

So the redefined goal is to lose 12 lbs in 8 weeks.

The next step would be the breaking down of the large goal into sub-goals. You could set yourself sub-goals of losing 1.5 lbs per week for the 8 weeks.

Make a table and post it on a wall so that you can see it. Suppose you weigh 12 stone now and want to lose the 12 lbs, your chart would look something like the one below:

GOAL: TO LOSE SOME WEIGHT

SPECIFICS: 12 lbs in 8 Weeks
WEIGHT AS AT xx/xx/06 = 12 Stone
TARGET WEIGHT AS AT xx/xx/06 = 11 Stone 2 lbs

	GOAL - LOSS	WEIGHT	ACTUAL
End of week 1	**1.5 lbs**	**11 stone 12.5 lbs**	
End of week 2	**1.5 lbs**	**11 stone 11 lbs**	
End of week 3	**1.5 lbs**	**11 stone 9.5 lbs**	
End of week 4	**1.5 lbs**	**11 stone 8 lbs**	
End of week 5	**1.5 lbs**	**11 stone 6.5 lbs**	
End of week 6	**1.5 lbs**	**11 stone 5 lbs**	
End of week 7	**1.5 lbs**	**11 stone 3.5 lbs**	
End of week 8	**1.5 lbs**	**11 stone 2 lbs**	

Losing 1.5 lbs a week does not look like a big deal, right?

Action Plan

What you have prepared is nothing but a well-defined, systematically divided goal. Now you need an action plan to achieve the goal. So, devise an exercise plan and a healthy diet to help you achieve your goal.

Brainstorm all of the actions you need to do in order to achieve this goal and chunk them into activities of similar nature.

For example:

Exercise – What exercises? How often? Do I need new kit? How much?

Diet – What food? How often? How many calories? Shopping List?

Type of gym – Locations? Prices? Clients?

You can also plan what exercise you are going to do on a particular day and how much time you are going to spend. Make another table, similar to the one you have already prepared, for your exercise routine and healthy eating plan. And always try to stick closely to the schedule.

The method used to illustrate the weight-loss example is often referred to as stair-stepping or chunking, which means breaking a big goal down into smaller components. By doing this, beside many other advantages, you can enjoy any number of successes even before achieving your final goal.

The stair-stepping method is similar to eating a Pizza!

Try to eat an entire pizza in one mouthful….no you can't. By

cutting it into smaller, bite-sized pieces you can make it more

eatable and more enjoyable.

Break your goals down and they will become a lot easier for you to

achieve. By focusing your attention on the comparatively easier

sub-goals, you can make great progress towards your final goal

without feeling overwhelmed.

If you concentrate on your sub-goals, your major goal will take care of itself.

GET THE TIMING RIGHT!

As Benjamin Franklin said

Never leave that till tomorrow which you can do today

Setting reasonable and realistic deadlines for each sub-goals as well as the final goal is very important. Putting things off until tomorrow or next week will turn into another tomorrow or another week.

Let's take a look at a word no aspiring successful person should have in his or her vocabulary. Meet **PROCRASTINATION!**

See how many ways it can affect your pursuit of success.

You could put things off by *never choosing to do anything.*

You could put things off by choosing to do something, *but you never start doing it.*

You could put things off by starting something, *but you never continue doing it.*

And then you could continue doing something, *but you never finish it.*

At every stage of your action plan you must set yourself deadlines so that you don't put things off until tomorrow.

DO NOT PROCRASTINATE

Breakdown your goal into a number of sub-goals

▼

Allot your time for each sub-goal

▼

Formulate deadlines to achieve each sub-goal and as well as the ultimate one

▼

Be honest in respecting your deadlines

This can be called the TIMETABLE TO SUCCESS.

Setting achievable and realistic goals and deadlines is very important. For example, one cannot expect to pass his/her driving test after only 2 lessons. Passing after 20 lessons is more attainable and realistic.

Never set a goal that exceeds your ability. However, at the same time, you need to ensure the maximum exploitation of the time allotted. The gap between potential and performance must be the minimum.

Success breeds success.

Setting realistic goals can help create the habit of achieving them. This will build up your confidence and help you attain more demanding goals. Moreover, by setting goals that are measurable and achievable, you can easily make corrections to them if you go off target.

If you are a manager or have people working for you, please bear the following in mind.

Setting unattainable targets or making unrealistic demands will only do harm to the motivation, self-esteem and confidence of your workforce and will result in a reduction in productivity.

If you ask too much of yourself, the same will happen to you as well. You will become de-motivated and will lose interest in doing it.

The most successful people in the world are those who can identify their own abilities and limitations. And the best managers are those who can identify their employees' abilities and limitations and then set work/goals that will stretch their abilities without exceeding the limit. Such managers invariably have highly motivated employees. Their approach makes the subordinates feeling worthwhile and encourages them to push the limits.

There is a fine line that divides goals that are too easy to achieve and goals that are probably out of reach. You can distinguish them by using your common sense, knowing your strengths and weaknesses, knowing your potential to develop and learn, and by using trail and error method.

You need to set specific goals for different areas of your life. You can set a goal that will help you take a leap in your career, or you can set a goal that will gain you personal rewards. Devise specific Action Plans and apply appropriate techniques in each case.

Following are some techniques and tips that you can use in setting goals and attaining them.

There is a saying, "A verbal contract isn't worth the paper it is written on."

It is of no good saying that you have got a goal if you haven't written it down. What you need is self-commitment, and writing things down is a start to developing it.

Setting Goals

An Example:

What?

Lose 10 lbs in weight

Why?

It will give me greater confidence, enhance my self esteem, and will make me more attractive to women

How?

Exercise, Diet, Allocating Time, Gym or home, etc

Chunking

1. Finding Gym, exercise routines, kit, frequency

    2. Nutrition

    3. Time Management and organization

Sub-goals

1. Lose 2 lbs per month
2. Buy 1 new item of clothing each month
3. Visit gym 4 times per week
4. Increase distance or resistance each time

Timelines

Major Goal attained within 5 months xx/xx/2011

X weight in 2 months yy/yy/2011

Review

What's going well? What are the results? Do I need to adjust?

Adjust

Make sure that you write everything down.

If you haven't already started formulating your goals, the following exercises will be helpful.

For each of your goals brainstorm and write down whatever you will need to achieve.

What will you need?

Are you experienced enough?

Who can help?

What will you have to do?

Is there a cost?

Do you need any equipment?

Do you require any capital?

Chunk all of the actions into 3 or 4 main areas and then class these as sub-goals. Give deadlines for each.

Then, GO FOR IT!

Achieving these goals will give you great self-confidence. It will also put you in the right frame of mind to achieve greater feats.

Other uses of goal attainment

The use of goal attainment should be a part of your daily routine.

If you are attending a course at work, determine what exactly you want to get out of it and why i.e. realize your goals and objectives.

If you have got an important interview, set yourself the goal of getting up an hour earlier to the usual time so that you can go through your notes once again.

If you are playing a round of golf and you shot a 75 last time around, set yourself the target of 73. And if you bench-pressed 200 lbs at the gym last time, try for 210.

Setting well-defined goals and achieving them in a systematic manner will increase your confidence and efficiency.

If you have staff to manage, give them realistic as well as demanding targets. No matter what their experience or expertise, you will get the best out of them. It will also help them improve their skills and productivity.

Think over the various points discussed in today's session. Go through your assignments again.

1 − 4

Overcoming Problems And Difficulties

**Obstacles are those frightful things you see
when you take your eyes off your goal.**

- Henry Ford

Welcome to chapter Four!

The way to success is no bed of roses. Whilst trying to attain your goals, there will be many obstacles in your way. You might face both physical and mental difficulties.

Instead of beating yourself up or giving in, you need to learn from setbacks. As you know, a diamond cannot be polished without friction.

Use obstacles and failures as an opportunity to polish your skills. You will have to sail with the wind sometimes, and sometimes against it. But, you must sail, and not drift nor lie at anchor.

So, what matters is your attitude. This session will have a look at your beliefs and let you know if you have got the attitude to thrive under pressure and to succeed.

Refocusing after setbacks

Edmund Hillary was three times unsuccessful while trying to climb Mount Everest before his historical achievement in 1953.

People praised his triumph and said, "You've conquered the mountain," and Sir Hillary said, "No, I've conquered myself."

The bitter experiences of early three attempts did not hold back Hillary from a fourth one. With strong will and relentless enthusiasm, he pursued his goal and achieved it.

How many times have you started a diet, stopped smoking, or tried something new and went back to where you were when a setback or obstacle occurred. People often stumble over obstacles and even consider them as excuses for their failures.

Setbacks and difficulties are inevitable in life. They often challenge your skills and temperament.

There are two ways to face difficulties.

1. You can either change the difficulty or change yourself to be able to deal with it.
2. You can deal with difficulties properly and make use of the experience to enhance your confidence or you can deal with them incorrectly and let them seriously damage your confidence.

If you can see and face challenges in a positive way, you will gain immense experience and knowledge from it. Remember, a smooth sea never made a skilful mariner.

Your response to issues and difficulties

Failure should never be considered as a source of discouragement, but a motivation. You know how Helen Keller, a mute and blind woman, went on to become a world-famous speaker and author. Your ability to deal with challenges can be converted into a virtue by asking positive empowering questions yourself.

There is an unwritten rule that says:

Ask your mind a stupid question and you will get a stupid answer!

So, if, after a setback, you ask yourself something like

"Why does this always happen to me, I never have any luck?"

Your mind will probably come out with:

"Because you are useless and good things do not happen to you!"

Instead, if you ask yourself a positive empowering question like:

"What did I learn from this setback for next time?"

Your mind will switch into solution mode and come out with some excellent tips.

Following are some points to ponder about when setbacks do occur:

- Be brave enough to acknowledge what has happened. Don't hide away from it. These things happen. So what?

- Ask yourself as many positive empowering questions as you can.

For example:
What is good about this situation?
How can I make the most of this situation?
What can I learn from it?
What are the facts about this problem?
How can we make it a success next time?

- Acknowledge the fact that setbacks occur to everyone and you are not being singled out.

- View setbacks as a challenge to overcome rather than an issue or problem.

Get your belief system right for success!

The pessimist sees the difficulty in every opportunity; the optimist sees the opportunity in every difficulty.

- Winston Churchil

It is difficult to get away from discouraging thoughts after a failure. Make a list of the negative thoughts and questions that usually come into your mind after a setback. Also think about the equally discouraging answers you normally have.

Then make a list of some encouraging questions you can ask instead. Obviously you also have some encouraging answers. Try to ask these encouraging questions every time you face a difficulty. Making it a habit can basically change your attitude to adversities.

How to Develop Strong Inner Beliefs

Development of a strong inner belief system is essential to avoid discouraging thoughts. You can clarify yourself by asking some self-assuring questions. Such clarifications will lead to self-acceptance, which, in turn, will give you the much needed energy and room to grow. Remember, He who conquers himself conquers the world.

Self-acceptance is all about how much one values, loves, and accepts himself/herself, rather than how much he/she feels valued, loved, or accepted by others. Having a strong value/inner belief system is very much dependent on your ability to accept yourself. So you need to accept your identity, your feelings and your outlook of the world.

The ability to appreciate one's own worth is a great virtue. People with healthy self-esteem are able to feel good about themselves and take pride in their skills and accomplishments.

People who consider themselves as having no admirable qualities may develop a low self-esteem. They may feel as if no one likes them or accepts them or they can't do well in anything. The problem becomes worse when someone whose acceptance is important constantly puts him/her down.

The benefits of a strong inner belief system are many;

- Stronger self-confidence
- Healthy self-esteem
- Greater life satisfaction
- Comfort with self and others

But how exactly does one go about developing a strong inner belief system?

Consider the following questions.

Finding answers to these can help you distinguish yourself in the group.

1. **Explore what you currently believe about work, life, people, and yourself.**

    You can try a free-writing exercise. Write each word (work, life, etc.) at the top of a page (one for each page) and then a free associate for each word. Write down whatever thoughts might be conjured up by the word at the top of the page.

    Write until each page is full.

2. **How much of what you believe is your own?**

    Take a look at what you wrote on each page.

    Identify messages that may have come from parents, friends, family, peers, teachers, etc. You can see that some thoughts appear under almost every section. Identify the recurring themes.

    Now, highlight the things that truly reflect who you are and what you believe.

3. **How much of it is enabling and how much disabling?**

    The messages of others can be encouraging or discouraging.

Now, look at the messages and thoughts that reflect your own inner belief system. How do they make you feel, empowering or limiting?

4.   What do you want to believe?

Consider your true beliefs, the thoughts and messages you firmly believe in.

Do they reflect how you want to feel about life, work, people, and yourself?

Take a blank paper and write down each idea or thought that are considered right by others on the left hand. On the right hand side write down your alternative; how you'd like to feel/think about each.

Reprogram yourself by identifying these limiting thoughts as they pop into your head, and replacing them with the thoughts and ideas you identified on the right hand side of the paper.

Continue this exercise, and you will find the old limiting thoughts creeping up less and less and the new empowering thoughts substituting them.

5.   What messages about life, people, work, and yourself did you get from family as you shaped your personality?

Family, your primary social unit, can influence you more than most other institutions.

Family members have the tendency to repeat their messages. If you have chosen to reprogram any of their thoughts, values or beliefs, then be prepared to counter these beliefs whenever a family member articulates them.

6. **What's your response when you express your belief and someone disagrees?**

There can be many who do not agree with your beliefs and ideas. Consider how you might respond, should you share your beliefs with others and find that they disagree.

You don't have to change your mind.

There is nothing wrong in someone else believing differently from your beliefs. People are different and that's what makes the world go round after all.

Simply convey that you see life/work/people/etc. differently, and then reconfirm your belief by repeating it to yourself.

As you explore your answers to these questions and the exercises associated with each, you'll begin to realize the strength of your inner belief system.

It is like the spirit that gives you life. You don't have to always experience or express its presence. It remains within you as long as you live.

Expression of an idea is a difficult job. You need a great amount of confidence to express your beliefs in an unwavering fashion. People will challenge you and come forward with counterarguments.

Consider it as an opportunity to test your ability to continue with your belief system intact as part of you own personal growth.

Once your belief system has been strengthened, you will find that others, having less confidence in their own beliefs, will seek you out. Also, never remain stagnant. You need to grow by helping and encouraging others to tap into their own belief system and follow the process you used.

That's it for this session.

1 – 5

How To Keep Motivated And Make The Changes

Welcome to chapter Five of How to Get What You Want!

After serious contemplation, the goals have been written down, broken into sub goals, actions plans have been charted, and you have started implementing the steps you have carefully planned...however...but....still...yet...there are those mixed feelings, distractions, or some stumbling blocks you are facing that's casting doubts...should I go on....is something wrong...

Here's Carol's experience along the lines given above, something you might easily correlate with. What did she do?

Carol Jenkins had enrolled for a German course. The objective behind doing that was simple. She was working at a firm, which had its corporate office in Germany. Employees with fluency in German get a chance to work at the corporate office for 6 months to one 1 year. An opportunity, if used properly could result in a promotion.

The language course was of 6 months duration, and it involved giving up on some precious weekend time both for classes and coping up with assignments. And, Carol was a very popular girl.

In the first month, everything went okay. But in the second month, those invitations she had been rejecting looked more and more appealing. In the third month, the German course became a royal pain. She was also not doing well in her classes.

Finally, her friend who had been silently observing her distress pointed out, "Do you really want the certification or not? If not, forget it. Better to waste three months than 6 months."

Carol's obvious response was, "You do not understand..............."

"Well, I might not but in the last month, you have been taking out your frustration on everyone around you. Your classes are also suffering. It's either letting go three months more of weekend fun or the German course. At this rate, I do not see you getting the certification. It requires an honest effort to study languages if nothing else," her friend replied.

It was decision time for Carol, and she understood. She opted for finishing the German course for the chance to work in Germany and the opportunity for promotion looked more attractive.

You need to be as committed and as motivated to work on them on the 5th, 6th, or 10th week as you were in the 1st.

There are all the probabilities that you might face setbacks.

More powerful deterrents than setbacks are those mixed feelings and temptations that seems to make you 'take things easy for a while' or procrastinate or simply slow down.

Have a look over the goals that you have written and the reasons why you want to achieve them.

Do they still give a tingle of excitement? Do they still mean a lot to you?

If they do not, then maybe the reasons behind achieving them were not compelling enough.

Check again whether your goals were 'Must Have's or 'Nice to Have's.

A list of MUST HAVE goals will give you the required focus to accomplish them in time. The real reason why people falter is because they have NICE HAVES on their lists.

"It would be nice to lose some weight"

"It would be nice to have a new job"

These NICE HAVES are not going to get you up early and keep you up late!

Here is a formula that will help you to change anything you want to and to get you to take action!

It will help you understand the forces at play while you are making a decision on whether changing or doing something is a 'must have' or 'nice to have.'

The Change Formula

There is a simple equation that you can apply to anything and everything while you are making a decision on whether you want to do something or not.

$$D \times V \times P > C$$

Where D stands for Dissatisfaction with the status quo

To make a visible positive change, you must be unhappy with the present situation.

V stands for Vision

This is another basic requirement. You must have a vision of the situation or position you want to achieve. And you must also have an idea of why you want it.

P stands for Practical steps

You must have an action plan of what you need to do. You need to be aware of each and everything you will have to change.

And C stands for Cost of changing

You must have an idea about what the changes will cost you. What will you have to sacrifice? Will you have to change your beliefs?

The **D**, **V** and **P** factors together form your desire to change.

However, the change will occur only if your desire is greater than the associated costs of changing **(C)**.

Here's something to give you a clearer picture.

The lecturer who first introduced us to this equation was a lovely and attractive, rather chubby lady.

As her name has to be kept confidential, let's call her Nancy.

Nancy narrated an incident in her life, which forms the basis of this formula.

Once, she had gone to visit the village where she had spent her childhood. She visited the local newsagent, where she used to buy sweets when she was younger.

The store-owner was the same person from whom she used to buy sweets 20 years ago.

Nancy was enthralled and asked him if he remembered her!

She helped him recall and he did, but the words that came out of his mouth left her baffled.

He said …..

"What an earth has happened to you? Haven't you let yourself go?"

You could very well imagine what a blow in the face Nancy would have felt as she left the shop!

Now, for most of us a harsh comment like that would sting and instigate us to take some serious action. It did for the lecturer too; she had the reasons and the required vision of what she would look like if she lost some weight.

She knew the practical steps and sacrifices she would need to make, like sessions at the gym and diet plans, to make the necessary changes.

But still she decided not to change.

Because,

SHE DID NOT HAVE ENOUGH MOTIVATION TO CHANGE

She weighed her options, scrutinized her priorities and realized that her cost of changing was much higher than her desire to change.

Nancy enjoyed her life as it was. Her diet consisted of traditional healthy and nutritious food, and she loved desserts. Though she did not over indulge, she could not imagine not having them at all. She loved partying.

The last thing she wanted to do was go to the gym every morning or evening, eat lettuce leaves or cabbages for dinner and breakfast, and then make herself starve after a hard day's work, when all she really needed was to wind down at home with a bottle of chardonnay.

We admire her immensely, for being true to herself and sorting out her priorities in life. There is a lot of pressure on people to be thin these days.

If she were to go ahead, and diet and exercise she would have become thin - but do you think she would have been happy?

We doubt.

She wasn't necessarily unhappy with her life. She chose her happiness over superficial gratification from the society which would have left her empty and miserable. She went where her heart was and came out a happier person.

This is exactly the approach we want you to follow, as you work out this formula for your goals.

As Anthony Robbins says

Achievement without Fulfilment is Failure!

For Hazel the cost of changing far outweighed what she was going to get in return.

People welcome making short term sacrifices to achieve a goal. But they tend to give up if it exceeds a limit, i.e. when the cost of changing is greater than the desire to change.

You need to identify the potential problems before you start working for a goal, by using methods like the Change formula.

Moreover, an unachieved goal could be another blow to your self-esteem. So, it's important to be well aware of the situation in advance and avoid giving up half way through.

People often comment, "I have no will-power." This probably means that they are enjoying something else and not what they are doing.

If you would be much happier without making the sacrifices, then making them would not be worth it.

Now, once again take a look at the things you have written down. Apply the formula whenever you find it difficult to take a decision.

SHOULD I CHANGE?

Remember

D x V x P > C

That's it for this session!

1 – 6

How To Live The Life You Want

The most important factor that goes into determining one's success is what goes on in his/her mind.

Where you are today and what you are today is because of your own mental attitude towards yourself and others. And you alone can change it. All that is needed is a change of your attitude.

The mental attitude that you carry is actually more important than it seems. It may be a boon or a bane for you. It could be affecting your life without your knowledge.

Your mental attitude could either take you up the path of success or down the depths of failure.

And changing it is only in your hands.

In this session, we shall see what the correct mental attitude actually is. Chances are that you already have it. But if you haven't, no worries!

You can always acquire it!

We already know how important motivation is and how it can work wonders in one's life. We shall further talk about this activity that gets you off your butt and kick starts you into action.

ATTITUDE – A LITTLE THING MAKES A BIG DIFFERENCE

It's not what happens to you that determine how far you will go in life; it is how you handle what happens to you.

– Zig Ziglar

Whatever you do in life, it is the attitude that you have before, during, and after doing it that determines your success or failure.

Now picture a footballer taking a penalty shot.

What do you think is going through his mind?

A goal?

Whether the goalkeeper will save it?

Or if the ball will end up somewhere in the row Z of the stand?

Driving lessons. I guess many of you would have gone for it. And got through as well. It is some pride to flaunt that driving license after having received it!

Now think of a person who has just failed his driving test. What thoughts will his mind be full of?

Confidence that he will pass it the next time he attempts?

A decision to quit bothering and give up?

A disheartened feeling that perhaps driving isn't meant for him and that he can be content with public transport?

There is but a simple rule that you should apply to your thinking in everything you do.

Think Positively and you will get positive results.

Think Negatively and you will get negative results.

It's as simple as that!

Ok, now that that's clear, complete this exercise.

The exercise will enable you to understand the thoughts of positive and negative people.

Think of the different people you know well – your friends, relatives and colleagues.

Classify all these people under two heads – negative thinkers and positive thinkers. As you know them well, this shouldn't be a very difficult task.

POSITIVE PEOPLE	NEGATIVE PEOPLE

There must be something which made you feel that they are positive-minded or negative-minded. Something that they said, or their reaction to something, etc.

In the box below, write out all those words that describe why you feel that the people under the heading 'positive people' are positive.

What do they say? How do they act? What do they do?

Now prepare another list. Here you have to classify the same people listed before into the two categories – successful and non-successful. Remember, it is your perception of whether they are a success or not.

SUCCESSFUL	NON-SUCCESSFUL

Now look at the two tables you have.

In all probability, you will find that most of the people you categorized as successful people are those who are positive-minded. Similarly, most of the people rated as unsuccessful will belong to the negative thinking lot!

Now you see!

Successful people in life are always positive people

They are the people who

- know what they want
- are optimistic
- expect the best
- expect to win

Negative people in turn, are pessimistic. They look for the worst in everything and expect to fail. These people tend to moan and complain a lot, and always try to put people down.

The way both positive and negative people handle problems is very different.

While positive-minded persons will look for solutions to the problems and a means to proceed further, the negative-minded persons will lose confidence. They will criticize themselves for having chosen that path and will be convinced that he is beaten even before he starts.

Everything that you choose to think, affects your life. The one thing that can bring success or failure in one's life is attitude.

Now think that you are a person who has come to attend an interview at an office.

Picture this.

You are sitting on one of those comfortable chairs outside the interview room in the office, your certificates and papers ready with you.

Now, what exactly is going through your mind as you sit there?

Let's look at it in two ways!

As a **negative-minded person**, you may think along the lines of – what on earth am I doing here? I haven't got any chance of getting this job. Neither do I have the required qualifications nor any experience. Most probably I will go in there and make a fool of myself in front of everyone. Why did I decide to come here at all?

As a **positive-minded person**, you will be confident and ready to face anything. You will probably think this way. If I have got this far, it is because of my own efforts. So I must be really good. And if I'm good, then I've got a great chance of getting the job. I have got the experience and qualifications and I will say only the right things when questioned. So I'm ready!

The thinking of both the persons is miles apart. The positive-minded person is confident and actually looking forward to attending the interview. In contrast, the negative-minded person is literally on the verge of running away. He doubts himself and dreads the approaching interview. The last thing he has is faith in himself.

Give a thought to this....

Which person do you think stands more of a chance of getting the job?

Put yourself in the shoes of the company boss. Which of the two people would you prefer working for you?

A positive mental attitude obviously boosts one's confidence. It gives the person a power that draws towards them the favorable circumstances, things and people that they think about the most.

Success is something everybody is after. But believe it or not, your attitude may actually be repelling the very thing you are after.

A positive mind attracts opportunities for success while a negative mind fends them off. In fact, a negative-minded person doesn't even take up the opportunities that come along. Why? He is busy focusing on the next time he is going to fail.

A SHORT CASE STUDY – When unemployed

Unemployment. Those who have been through it will know. It's a terrible!

Neville did not have a job. Neither did he have any money. There were numerous jobs that he wasn't even applying for as he was sure that he stood no chance in getting them.

He had the mindset of a loser. He had what we just saw to be a negative mind.

Finally he decided to change himself. He made it a point to think positively in all situations. And what a difference that made! His life changed!

The glass that was once looked half empty to him now seemed half full.

The results were amazing. Neville started to radiate confidence and optimism instead of the usual feelings of self-pity and failure. This attracted the right kinds of people to him. With all the pieces of the puzzle put together, success just had to come to him.

So you see the connection?

Positive-thinking → Success

Suppose you are at a party.

What kind of people would you be drawn towards in a party?

Would it be.....

- a good-humored person who looks at things positively and spreads laughter?

OR

- a miserable looking person who has nothing to talk about but depressing things?

Doesn't require much thinking does it?

Another valuable lesson you could do with is this:

You may find yourself in a difficult situation sometimes, but then don't forget that someone else could be in a much worse situation.

Frank was the only son of his parents. It was Christmas and he expected them to buy a new pair of shoes for him. But his parents could not afford anything at that time. He complained and said such words as "you don't care about me at all" and walked out of the house. Angry as he was, he kicked at everything he saw on the path. Suddenly he stopped in his tracks. He saw before him a man without any feet! It dawned upon him how lucky he was. "What if I don't have new shoes, am I not lucky to have my two feet?"he told himself. His parents were glad to find their son happy and not complaining anymore when he came back.

This is a story you might have heard before in different forms. Doesn't it convey a simple message? Look at what you have instead of what you don't have.

Whatever your mind can conceive and believe, your mind can achieve.

- **Napoleon Hill**

Your greatest potential asset is your ability to believe.

The only problem is that you can't benefit from it unless you have what is required- a positive attitude.

You earlier saw that successful people are positive people.

Now ask yourself this-

Am I one of them? Do I think positively?

No matter what mindset you have, there are ways to change it. There are techniques that you could apply to cultivate positive habits in yourself.

You can learn them all....right here!

These techniques have helped people form and keep a positive mental attitude. It has bettered their lives. If it worked for them, why won't it work for you?

Coming up is a bit of practical advice that you could very well act upon. You may be an unemployed person desperately looking for a job or even the Managing Director of a company. The suggestions are recommended for everyone to apply in their life.

How to Form and Keep a Positive Mental Attitude

To get e positive mental attitude, first of all what you need to do is think and act on the "CAN DO" approach of every activity instead of the "NO CAN'T DO" approach.

Positive people look for answers while negative people look for questions.

There's a poem by Joyce.C. Lock, which has these lines

If I were a hammer, I'd miss the nail

If I were a knife, I'd cut a finger as well

If I were a letter, I'd be lost in the mail

There are many more such lines in is poem but I can't recollect. Do you also think on such lines? Are you a problem seeker or a solution seeker?

The negative persons are, in short, problem seekers. They believe that problems and obstacles cannot be surpassed. As against that, positive people, no matter what problem they are facing, look for solutions.

All it takes is a smile!

Go back to the lists about positive and negative people that you had created before. Look at the positive people listed on it.

Mull over this:

Don't these people smile and laugh a lot more and appear happier than the negative thinkers?

It may seem very silly, but there is a lot of power associated with a smile. A smile is always returned with a smile.

So now onwards, follow this rule - **Smile more often!**

That doesn't mean you have to walk around with a silly grin on your face all the time. Smile when you speak to someone, smile as you walk down the street, smile when looking at yourself in the mirror, smile even when speaking on the phone.

You will be amazed by the good feeling that it generates within you. You feel better and project a positive image to others, which attracts opportunities and more people towards you.

Remember, positive people are happy people and negative people are not.

Happy people seem to be more attractive and pleasant to others compared to gloomy people. Isn't this an added bonus for you?

Pat people on the back

Maria had got a very good position at a local firm. Though the work was something she enjoyed doing, she was never satisfied. Her boss never appreciated her work. She worked very hard and received a lot of appreciation from her colleagues. However her boss merely looks at the work and grumbles. She had been feeling down since she joined till her colleagues confided in her that the man was like that. He never appreciated good work. Instead there was no end to his criticism.

There are many people we see in life who jump at the chance of criticizing a person when something goes wrong. Moreover, these people don't even acknowledge you when you are right!

To create and reflect a positive mental attitude, start complimenting people. If you already have the habit, increase the number of times you do it.

If your partner buys a new piece of clothing and looks attractive, don't just notice that. Tell them so!

You don't lose anything by complimenting someone, do you? And anyway, a compliment never goes waste.

So, compliment your staff and colleagues on their work.

Compliment your child on making it to the football team.

The general idea is that you feel good by making others feel good and it enhances your Positive Mental Attitude. What more, you also enhance the Positive Mental Attitude of the people you compliment!

Merely complimenting people is not enough. The way we treat them is also important. Just follow this simple rule:

Treat others as we would like to be treated ourselves

This involves treating everyone as though he/she is the most important person in the world- because to him or her it stands true!

The laws of Success state that whatever you hand out in life, you get back at least ten times as much of it.

Connect this rule to life. If you make other people feel worthwhile, useful and valuable, you too are bound to be treated in the same manner- ten times as much.

Research has shown that a customer will tell at least ten people if his expectations from a company have been met with or exceeded, or even if his complaint was dealt with promptly and efficiently.

The same happens if you exceed the expectations of your friends, your boss and your colleagues. You will find yourself becoming popular, highly regarded and noted.

Now comes a warning.

When you compliment people and treat them with respect, be sure that you are doing so genuinely. You must mean what you say.

Believe, conceive and achieve

Start believing that success to you is inevitable.

Whatever task you are given, picture success in your mind. Burn the thought into your subconscious mind. Keep yourself focused on the outcome that you want to achieve in what you do. The mind can achieve anything that it believes and conceives.

You will be surprised to know that there is a giant asleep within yourself. You can direct him to do anything that you want.

You have no idea what you are capable of. Don't underestimate yourself. Believe it, the power of your mind and imagination is truly exceptional.

You can think your way to almost anything in life - success, happiness, illness and even death.

Read this small story.

Willy was a middle-aged man who was working in a refrigeration unit in America.

One day he somehow got himself locked inside the unit accidentally. He banged on the door, he screamed for some time, but no one heard him. He gave up.

Willy sat down defeated and was sure that he was going to die soon. He became all numb and cold. He somehow scribbled a message for the people who would eventually find him.

"Getting colder now, starting to shiver, nothing to do but wait, slowly freezing to death, half asleep now these are my final words".

At least five hours passed before someone opened the door and found the dead man's body.

Now that's a sad story. Here comes the twist.

The temperature inside the unit was 56 degrees. All day, the unit had been broken, thereby letting in enough air. Willy simply lost hope. Had he tried, he could have survived because there was plenty of air for him to breathe.

Realize that your mind can't distinguish between thoughts and reality. If you feed it with negative thoughts, your mind will mistake it as something that is actually happening. This is what happened with Willy. He wrote his own death.

Remember those times when you are at home all alone. You seemed to hear every bump, grind and creak clearly, isn't it? Didn't you feel that the clock was ticking very loudly and the tap was dripping like never before?

The same sounds, you would never have heard if you had company!

Why does that happen?

Because your mind is expecting to hear them.

Rehearsal practice- "You've succeeded before you have even begun"

Get yourself introduced to what is called Rehearsal practice. This is an important technique that can enhance your positive mental attitude.

Use the power of your mind to get better results. Put to use that awesome power of imagination that could be now rusting away.

Whatever situation you are put to, rehearse it over once in your mind. Believe it, if you play it over in your mind before you do it better.

By doing so, you are training your subconscious to behave in a certain way to obtain the result that you so much desire.

Let's go back to the job interview.

If you go over in your mind what the interview will probably be like, you can be more prepared. You could imagine things the kind of questions going to be asked, the possible scenario in the interview room, etc. With this done, you will be ready for whatever the interviewer throws at you.

You can use this method in anything that you do. It applies to everything from a driving test to a presentation to hitting a golf shot. Rehearsal practice is also called visualization. It is another form of focusing on the desired outcome.

Before a presentation you could imagine yourself doing the presentation, tackling the questions that the audience asks. You can have a look at possible questions and be well prepared.

Prior to a speech you could imagine it happening at the venue.

If you have a party at home, let the party happen once in your mind.

In all cases you will realize if you have missed out on anything.

That's visualization! It really helps!

If you have a driving test, you could think about all the possible road junctions that you may have to cover as a part of the test and picture yourself successfully completing them. Also think over the questions that you will probably be asked.

You will see that you can attend the test brimming with confidence. And most probably, the other people will be dreading it. In your mind, you will already have passed the test and so you will confidently look forward to it.

So start today, from right now!

Mentally rehearse or visualize any situation that you find challenging.

Look at athletes on television before a big race or long jump. They will be mentally preparing themselves and going over and over in their mind how they will run or jump. They will be visualizing themselves succeeding.

Apply visualization to the goals in your life. Take 5 minutes of your day for them. Close your eyes and think that you have already achieved the goals. Picture what your life is like, now that you have achieved your goals (in your mind).

You will be fascinated by the end-results.

Now in the midst of all this positive thinking, what if a negative thought creeps in?

Rachel was preparing for a presentation that she was to do before a very important client. Winning the client was very important for her company. All hopes were on her. She was always very confident and that was mainly why she was given the task. The pressure of everybody's expectations was weighing down on her. And yet it didn't seem to affect her. She had thought over the presentation many times in her mind and had won the client.

Once or twice, negative thoughts like 'what if I forget what I have to say?'; 'what if I'm not able to answer some question the client asks?' seeped in. She brushed them all aside with poise and told herself she had it in her to do well.

What more was needed? She did her best in the presentation and won the client.

So what do you have to do when a negative client finds its way into your mind?

Stop right there, get rid of the negative thought and replace it with a positive thought.

That's easier said than done- you will say.

Ok, try this way. Tell/ask yourself the following every time you experience a negative thought:

"Is this thought really important in the grand scheme of things?"

"What can I change about this thought to make it positive?"

"Think back through past experiences that have been worse and put this thought into the picture"

"Why did that person say what he said? What was behind it? They probably have the problem, not me."

Focus on success and watch, as the people, opportunities
and outcomes come your way

Most attributes used to describe a winner are those that can be seen in first class salespeople.

Think of any salesman in any shop or anywhere. If he talks nicely to you and takes care of your requirements, you will say he is nice. Many times you end up buying a product only because of the person.

Salesmanship has got a lot to do with attitude. Whatever we do in life, we are selling ourselves or something, and a person with a negative mindset can sell nothing.

Don't believe it?

What do you think you are doing at an interview, during a presentation, while talking to someone or even when you are on a date?

Yes, you are selling yourself! And that requires you to be positive.

You need a positive attitude to attain your goals. Even for growth, development and progress in life you need a positive mind.

In the journey called life, you have to maintain a positive attitude when faced with opposition from other people or adverse situations.

If you don't have a Positive Mental Attitude, you usually end up being a loser.

If you remain positive and make sure that you are not susceptible to the negative influences of other people- YOU WILL SUCCEED.

Remember this:

All of the world's most successful people have had setbacks in their quest for success.

Consider Richard Branson's lottery bid failure and his hot-air balloon crash or the difficult phases in his career that Ian Botham had endure.

Both of these legends have everything that is required for a positive mental attitude. They have the skill and confidence to get up from any fall, dust themselves down and carry on regardless.

Your success is not about how many times you fall. It's about how many times you pick yourself after falling. Only persistence can take you to success.

Negative minded people would have given up at these junctures. But Branson and Botham went on to bigger and better things.

It was all thanks to their POSITIVE MENTAL ATTITUDE.

In Botham's own words – "Erase failure from your mind and you will be surprised how little you do fail" - that is the attitude of a truly successful person, one which we should adhere to.

In Summing Up

Without a positive attitude you will find it difficult to achieve anything in life.

Remember, it is your attitude that determines your success.

People who are negative-minded never get anywhere. They are invariably unsuccessful.

Throughout this topic we have seen the advantages of a Positive Mental Attitude. Make sure that you implement these techniques in your life right away!

Think positively and the world is your oyster.

Think negatively and you are doomed to failure.

Any hesitation on what to choose? No way!

MAXIMIZING YOUR POTENTIAL

It is important that you know your goals in life. We have already seen the importance of goal setting and goal attainment. It is vital that you know what you want to do with your life and where you want to go.

You should also know what kind of person you want to be as well.

The way you look, your attire, your possessions, what you say and how you say it, etc – everything goes into determining whether you are successful.

You will be and feel your best when you are winning. So care to look your best too!

Most successful people/winners constantly try to improve areas of their total presentation. They understand and accept that it is a vital factor that helps them maximize their potential.

Now, there is something that you should understand here.

Don't mistake the tendency of these people to change such aspects of their life as something that stems from a feeling of inadequacy or inferiority.

A feeling of inadequacy is by no means the reason for winners and successful people making improvements in their appearance and other areas of their life.

These people are confident about themselves, and know that they are brilliant in their own way. Yet they keep trying to improve even further.

Self Image

You will have a mental perception of how you would like others to see you and what type of a person you would like to be. It is important that you have such a picture of yourself.

The self-image that you show everyone is supposed to be the external result of your internal self-esteem.

You must be meeting plenty of people in your everyday life. Now think over.

How many of them have you seen who walk around with their head bent low and back crouched?

What image do you feel is conveyed about their self-esteem?

Do you think they would be able to sell themselves?

The very impression they project is that of a loser. A person who fears challenges and is not confident about himself.

In contrast, winners present a dignified presence to the world.

Self-belief seems to radiate from winners. They are confident and walk tall. Their very manner lets people know "I am a good person. I deserve to be respected."

Not everyone will agree when it is said that one's appearance is as importance as his attitude. Appearances count a lot in today's society.

Losers don't give much importance to appearance. They make no move to change and want to be accepted as they are.

However it is not what you look like that counts. It is how you feel about your looks that affects your confidence and self-esteem.

To bring out the best in you, it is important that you feel good about yourself, what you are and what you do. You should be happy with yourself. Only then will you radiate the confidence, energy and enthusiasm that form a vital part of success.

If you are not satisfied with yourself, there will be something holding you back from touching the shores of success – a low self-esteem.

If you have no confidence in self, you are twice defeated in the race of life. With confidence, you have won even before you have started

- Marcus Garvey

If you carry a good-feeling about yourself you believe that others also will like you the way you are. If you project the image that you are likeable, obviously people will like you.

In short, it is impossible for you to feel confident and assured unless you love and respect yourself.

Someone once said:

A man who loveth himself right will do everything else right

A healthy self-image along with the associated feelings of competence, confidence and worth is essential to impress a positive image of yourself on others.

The feel good factor

Let us first of all understand what the 'feel good factor' is.

Have you ever had a bad hair day?

A time when, no matter what you do to it, the damn thing will not go into place?

You comb it, brush it and dampen it – all to no avail.

It remains as stubborn as ever.

Now, think back. What was your mood like later? How did you feel that whole day?

Down?

Low on confidence?

Short of self-esteem?

Another question for you.

Think of a complete opposite situation to the 'bad-hair day'.

A time when you've just had your hair done

Or

Just bought a new suit

How do you feel then?

Confident?

A million dollars?

Ready to take on anything?

The feel good factor is such a positive force that it can influence your whole life.

Now suppose that on the very day that you are low and irritated you are called into the Managing Director's office. This comes as a rare chance for you to impress the most important person in the organization and somehow it had to come just at a time when your confidence is not at its best.

Will this help or hinder your performance?

Beyond doubt, hinder!

Erase this image of yourself. Now think of a time when you are wearing one of your favorite suits, your hair is perfectly set and you are feeling confident and sharp and your energy levels are high.

What if you get the call to the M.D's office now? Wouldn't you grab the opportunity to prove yourself? Brimming with confidence, as you would be, nothing will be difficult for you!

So what do you infer?

You must put yourself in a position where you feel confident that you can take on anything to maximize your potential in life.

If you are not happy with your appearance and the things around you, your self-esteem and confidence are affected. The two of them are some of the most important things that determine your performance.

The feel good factor and the feel bad factor are millions of miles apart from each other. What goes without saying is that you must try to inculcate the feel good factor in your life.

How to get it into your life is something that only you will know, as it concerns your life. It will give you that great confidence to perform and excel in everything that you do. And if you do have this factor, success will be handed to you on a plate.

We have already seen what the pros and cons of self-esteem, both high and low, are.

You will in the coming pages see some techniques that will help you boost your self-esteem level and confidence.

In the end, hopefully you will have a better perception of yourself and a good idea of the areas that you have to improve on.

RAISING YOUR SELF-ESTEEM

First of all let us try to get an idea about how you think other people perceive you. Complete the sentences below with one or two paragraphs. Be as honest as you can:

When a person sees or meets me for the first time they think...

When a person sees or meets me for the first time I would like them to think that...

These are two critical questions that bring to light couple of facts about you – how you think others perceive you and how you want them to perceive you.

Look at what you have written above. If what you want others to think about you and what you feel they presently think about you are the same, then it's a real good sign! That would mean you are what you want to be and people perceive you the way you want to be perceived.

That denotes an extremely high self-esteem.

Now if this is not the case, there are differences between the two, then there are areas that you need to work on. Your self-esteem would have to be given that extra lift.

Write down the differences that you found between what you feel others think about you and what you feel they think. Also make a brief statement of how you can improve them.

Some cases would require significant improvements. It may require a diet, exercise and/or grooming. Other minor improvements that some people could do with are in the way they shake hands with others and their ability to remember names.

Now please write down all those characteristics of the person you consider as the ideal person and whom you would like to become like.

Write down everything about this person. The looks, the hair, the kind of clothes he/she wears, mannerisms, his/her car, etc. Don't miss out on any detail, no matter how small it may be.

Done the exercise?

Now ask yourself this question.

Do you prefer his or her life to your own?

If you do, start to write down what you can do to close the gap:

Regularly doing this exercise will enable your development as a person and will ensure that you will not be distracted from.

No matter what your list says, let us now look at some of the most common areas of personal development. They may not comply to you now but will surely help you in one way or the other in life.

We have already seen how important the feel good factor is in one's life.

To enhance this factor, begin with examining every area of your appearance.

You could perhaps buy an image consultancy book that includes such things as the types and shades of clothing that complement your face and complexion, the hairdo that would bring out the best in your facial features, the most appropriate frame for your glasses to suit your face.

Image consultancy books act as the perfect guide to feeling and looking your best with style, grooming and wardrobe tips.

They enhance your confidence and make you feel great.

Why, you could take one step further and have an actual image consultation.

Looks apart, your possessions are another area that influence your self-esteem.

What you can do is produce a list once a month of the possessions that you would like to have. The contents of the list can be further broken down into three.

The example below would give you a better idea.

1. Items that I can go out and purchase immediately:

E.g. a tie, cufflinks, a shirt

2. Items to buy which I would have to save a little

E.g. a suit, a CD system, a computer

3. Items that require long term savings

E.g. a car, a house, a luxury holiday

Medium and long term savings plans can then be created to acquire the items listed in 2 and 3 above. Meanwhile you can treat yourself to at least two items per month that form part of 1.

As a result, the smaller possessions will make you feel good. And when you finally buy the larger possessions that need saving, you feel even better!

You will by now have a good idea of what you have to look like, own and possess in order to feel your best.

You could be the most confident person in the world or the least. But there is room for improvement in everyone's life.

It may sound amusing, but in order to make a positive impact on others you should have a love affair yourself. In short, you should feel good about yourself. Because if you feel so, it is apparent to everyone you meet.

If you feel bad about your shape, physique, clothes, grooming, manner or appearance, it will be much harder for you to remain confident and assured in social situations.

Someone once asked:

If you treated your friends like you treated yourself, would you have any?

You are your own best friend because wherever you go, your best friend goes with you. He/she is always there with you when you need it. Keep that in mind and remember to be nice to yourself.

The way we treat ourselves has a direct impact on how others will treat us.

The way you treat yourself can work as a means to show others how they should treat you.

Consider this case.

Andy treats himself really well. Everything about him reflects confidence. He eats in the best of restaurants, he has expensive suits and makes sure that he is well groomed always.

Thanks to this, whenever his friends know that he is coming to their place, guess what they do!

Yes, they tidy up the house, buy his favorite bottle of wine, etc. This happens only because they know how he treats himself. As he treats himself well, they also tend to treat him the same way.

Become Your Own Best Friend and Everyone Else Will Treat You Like Theirs

We had earlier seen the importance of complimenting other people. It is equally important to put yourself in the position whereby you receive the compliments.

Look at yourself.

Are you happy with the way you dress? If yes, then it's great!

But if you are not happy, buy the clothes that you feel will make you feel good.

What about other things - your house, your car, garage and office desk? Are they in a mess? Well then, tidy them up.

You wonder what that has got to do with self-esteem. Fair question.

Okay, think about this.

What if someone new got into your car and there were papers, cans, grit and other stuff lying around? What do you think this says about your self-esteem?

Not anything good, definitely!

Are you happy with your weight? If yes, that's good for you. People like you are a very rare find.

But if you aren't happy, go on an exercise and healthy eating plan.

MAKE PEOPLE SAY

"WOW! YOU LOOK GREAT!"

So many things depend on the level of your self-esteem. It is one thing that can either open many doors for you or shut them tight.

When it comes to those few moments of truth in your life - that 20 minute promotion presentation or that 10 minute chat to the M.D, you must be at your best and feel your best so that you can perform your best.

When you are feeling good about yourself, you feel you can conquer anything. It is a time when no obstacle is too great and no mountain is too steep to climb, for you.

Your self esteem can be improved by internal (thoughts about yourself) and external (appearance, possessions) factors.

To maximize your potential in life you must analyze your SELF-ESTEEM.

Try to put yourself in a position where both your mind and body are one. And remain there.

Once you have achieved this you will know because you will never have felt anything like it - THE POWER OF A HIGH SELF-ESTEEM AND THE CONFIDENCE TO ACHIEVE ALMOST ANYTHING.

So that's it!

Thanks for your continued support.

Remember what you learned. Work out what you want, how you want it and how you will get it and then decide what kind of a person you need to become to get it!

Success is all about common sense, but unfortunately, common sense is not common.

If at any time, you feel the need to have some one-to-one coaching, do call.

Section 2
Unstoppable Confidence
Getting the Poise That Spells Success

Introduction

"If you think you can, you can. And if you think you can't, you're right", said Henry Ford, the founder of the Ford Motor Company.

No wonder this confident man put the wheels of modern automobiles in motion and also acted as a powerful catalyst in the 20th century economy and society.

In today's world that so strongly emphasizes the importance of self-confidence, the modern man has no choice but to spruce up his confidence levels or he'll be left far behind in the rat race and never be able to rise above it.

"Unstoppable Confidence" is 6 parts that will help you improve on and raise those confidence levels just the way you want.

Through this module you will participate in exciting exercises and assignments, which are more than just learning experiences.

"Unstoppable Confidence" will help you break through all barriers and fixed notions you have about yourself and life in general and move forward in life.

Confident people are successful people. They stick it out till they get what they want. This is because they confidently believe in their goals and their own ability.

If you are reading this now, you are aware that a lack of confidence has seriously held you back in achieving the important goals of your life. It is time you do away with your misgivings and lack of self-belief.

You don't want to be timid and quiet when the world around you is confident and brimming with life, do you? So, fight the coyness and get what you want - SELF-CONFIDENCE! The Unstoppable kind...

2 – 1

Just How Confident Are You?

Take the assessment and all will be revealed!

Rona Tyrrell was a member of a women's spirituality group at her church. At 43, she was shy to speak up with friends, or in groups. During a convention on seniors activity group Rona was unexpectedly asked to speak to the members. After the initial panic and fear, she slowly found herself relaxing. Deep breaths and pep talk on the way to the pulpit worked! She was finally able to give an anxiety-free talk to the group.

Rona Tyrrell was taking a confidence building course at the time and was 2 weeks into it.

Or let's take the case of Peter Malloy. 24 year old Peter was a skilled graphic designer and though his resume exhibited his credentials, he could never really voice them. Since most jobs required him to interact with clients, he failed to make an impression on prospective employers due to his lack of communication skills and self-confidence. Luckily, Peter enrolled himself in a confidence building course and within a few weeks got through an interview at an international firm.

Now isn't that a very positive note to start a Confidence Building course?

You agree?

Great!

This module is all about self-discovery. Unless you know where you are, how will you move to where you want to be?

Before we begin confidence building exercises that will work on areas where you need more confidence, take these 2 assessment tests below.

Self-assessment

****

Rate the following statements from 0 – 10 based on how much you believe each of them to be true.

➢ 0 would mean that you don't believe in the statement at all and that it's utter nonsense.

➢ 10 would mean you think it's completely true.

****

Statements
****

- ◆ I like myself as a person
- ◆ I am as good as everyone else
- ◆ When I look at myself in the mirror I like what I see
- ◆ I don't feel like an overall failure
- ◆ I am happy to be me
- ◆ I respect myself
- ◆ I'd rather be me than anyone else
- ◆ What others say to me has no affect
- ◆ I enjoy communicating to others
- ◆ I have the skills and qualities to make myself a success
- ◆ I like to take risks
- ◆ I am not afraid to make mistakes
- ◆ I can laugh at myself

Now sum up all your scores.

Want to know where your confidence level stands?

Here goes...

If you have scored:

100 – 130

You have a high level of self esteem and confidence. All you have to do is fine tune it and increase your confidence in a couple of areas.

65 – 99

You have a medium to high ranking in self esteem. Whilst most of the time you are okay, there are times when you can feel rock bottom. You need more consistent feelings that you are confident and learn to experience these more regularly.

30 – 64

You have low levels of self esteem.

You lack confidence in yourself in most areas and need to have an overall confidence building plan.

0 – 29

You have reached rock bottom and think that everything and everyone is against you. You are stuck in a rut and need to get out of it quick

So, what are your scores like? Are they satisfactory, or are you hiding them under the couch?

Hold it, if you are! There's nothing to hide or feel ashamed about.

What you could do is write down some of the observations you made along this assessment.

What do you specifically need to concentrate on with regards to building up your confidence?

After you have written these down, take a look at the 'Confidence Evaluator' in the attachment. This is a test to make you fully aware of what you need to work on.

Complete the test fully and look at your scores in each section.

What do you notice?

It is not in every area of your life where you need confidence, only some.

Please get these down – the first step to improving anything is knowing where you are currently at.

Okay, so that's it for this session.

Assess yourself with the 'Confidence Evaluator' and see how you do.

2 – 2

Controlling Your Beliefs

Have you completed the "Confidence Evaluator" by now?

What were your scores like?

What you can do now is write down what 2 things you would love to master with regards to your confidence.

With the upcoming exercise you will begin to create the person that you want to become in terms of confidence.

The secret of success here lies in a visual image of how you would want to act, walk, talk, think and move your body so that you know what to aspire for.

Remember that we are working with confidence set as our goal!

And like any other goal you want to achieve, this one too should be clear because you should know what you are after and how you are going to get it.

The next step to confidence is if your self-esteem reaches rock bottom, what should you do? Think of your CONFIDENCE ROLE MODEL and ask yourself:

"How would my confidence role model deal with this situation?"

When you have your answer, do just as your role model did. This might feel weird in the beginning, but it will do you loads of good.

PRACTICAL

Moving on, there must be someone whose confidence levels you admire a lot; a colleague, friend, someone in your family or even a famous personality who oozes self-confidence; someone who has high self-esteem and therefore you admire.

Think about this person if you would like your confidence levels to boost up just like him or her.

On the other hand, this is your chance to start from scratch- to improve the way you walk, talk, and think; and your body language on the whole.

Ponder, ponder, ponder; long and hard.

You have to now fill out the following sections. But make sure the person whose confidence levels you admire is really worth that admiration.

MY CONFIDENCE ROLE MODEL

He/she would act like...

He/she would talk like...

He/she would walk like...

He/she would think like...

Their body language would be like...

Other people think that this person is...

When faced with problems, this person thinks...
Now take note of the few things you have written down about your confidence role model. The idea is to make an effort to be like you desire to be. So let's start with the basics.

Put these qualities into action. Yes! You heard it right.

ACT AS IF YOU ARE THE PERSON YOU WANT TO BE AND NOTICE THE RESULTS.

Don't worry if this feels awkward, because it will! After all you are acting out what you are really not. It will take a while for it to sink within and feel normal.

You will also need a strong inner belief system to be the confident person you want to become. Self-acceptance gives you the much needed energy and room to grow. Your inner belief system helps you develop an ability to accept yourself – who we are, what we feel, think and do.

The benefits of a strong inner belief system are varied and great:

- ◆ Stronger self confidence
- ◆ Healthy self esteem
- ◆ Greater life satisfaction
- ◆ Comfort with self and others

But how is this inner belief system developed?

Consider the following questions. Finding the answers to these can help you to weed out the **muck** of what "everybody else says" and get back to the purity and perfection of self-expression.

1. What are your current beliefs about work, life, people, and about yourself? Let go and try a free-writing exercise.

- On top of a page write one word (work, life, etc, - one for each page) and then free associate for each word.

- Write down whatever thoughts might be conjured up by the word at the top of the page.

- Write until each page is full!

2. How much of what you believe is your own?

- Take a look at what you wrote on each page.

- What messages may have come from parents, friends, family, peers, teachers, etc?

- Identify the recurring themes?

- Now, pick out and highlight the things you feel truly reflect who you are and what you believe.

3. How much of it is enabling versus disabling?

- Are the messages that came from others enabling and empowering? Or are they limiting?

- Now, look at the ones that reflect your own inner belief system-are those empowering or limiting?

- How do they make you feel?

4. What do you want to believe?

- Mull over your true beliefs.

- Do they reflect how you want to feel about life, work, people and yourself?

- Write each idea or thought down on the left hand side of a page, and on the right hand side, write how you'd like to feel/think about each instead.

- Reprogram yourself by identifying these limiting thoughts as they pop into your head, and replacing them with the thoughts and ideas you identified on the right hand side instead.

- If you continue this exercise, you'll find the old limiting thoughts creeping up less and less, and the new empowering thoughts will begin to take their place.

5. What messages about life, people, work and yourself did you get from family as you shaped your personality?

- Be prepared.

- Messages from family members are repetitive and will keep coming up.

- If you have chosen to reprogram any of their thoughts, values and beliefs, then be prepared to counter these beliefs whenever a family member articulates them.

6. What's your response when you express your belief and someone disagrees?

- How are you going to respond should you share your beliefs with others, and find that they disagree?

- Here's a hint: don't change your mind. It's okay that someone else believes differently from you-that's what makes the world go round after all.

- Instead, simply state that you see life/work/people/etc. differently, and then repeat and reconfirm your belief to yourself.

These questions, their answers and the exercises associated with each are sure to strengthen your belief system. Just like your soul that gives you life, you don't have to reinforce or communicate your belief. Nevertheless its presence is undisputed.

Your challenge is to develop confidence in your ability to express these beliefs in an unwavering fashion.

There are sure to people who will disregard your beliefs. What you have to do is test your ability to continue with your belief system and keep it intact as a part of your personal growth. If it continues to feel solid, then restate and reinforce it strongly.

Moving ahead, in the process, once your belief system has been strengthened, you will find that those having less confidence in their own beliefs will seek you out.

You can now help and encourage others and tap them into your own belief system, following the process you used to get where you are now.

Well then, what are you waiting for?

Start now!

2 – 3

How To Overcome Negative Thoughts

Even the most positive person gets negative thoughts!

Yes, that's true.

Olympian John Konrads won one gold and one bronze medal in the 1960 Rome Olympics. During the 400-meter freestyle, for which Konrads won the bronze medal, he said he lost focus by nurturing negative thoughts on how arch rival Murray was going to perform. Konrads confessed that though he had convinced himself he could win, these thoughts got in the way and blew his chances.

Actually, negative thoughts are commonplace and anyone can be a 'victim' to them. However, it's not the presence of negative thoughts but the way we handle and react to them that either breaks or makes our confidence and self-esteem.

Think over this:

NOTHING HAS ANY MEANING IN LIFE,

ONLY THE MEANING YOU GIVE TO IT.

If you ALLOW negative thoughts to HARM you – THEY WILL!

If you ALLOW negative thoughts to HELP you – THEY WILL!

Before we get into this session it's important to keep a few points in mind:

+ It's not only you that gets negative thoughts; everyone on this planet gets them.
+ You are not making an attempt to uproot negative thoughts here. Just handling them more smartly.
+ Negative thoughts, as such, do not harm you. It's what you say to yourself after the thought has entered your head that harms you.

♦ You can change any thought you want by changing what it means to you.

With that taken into account, let's kick off this session!

Analyzing your thoughts

Want to increase your confidence? You have to first find out what triggers off those negative thoughts and emotions you have about yourself.

It becomes easier to analyze and respond to them if you write them down.

FYI, it is not the trigger or the event that instigates the bad feelings. What make you feel despondent are the internal dialogues you say to yourself in response to the trigger.

These catalysts distort reality and put your feelings in turmoil.

That's the kind of turmoil Lynette got into. Her husband Roger had been quite distracted over the past few days. Lynette tried talking to him on a couple of occasions but he wasn't forthcoming. She heard him talking in hushed tones over the phone, and he also came home late more often than before. Lynette was perturbed beyond words. She spent hours talking to herself, wondering what Roger was up to.

She would have said:

- ♦ **"He's ignoring me."**
- ♦ **"Maybe he's having an affair with someone."**
- ♦ **"He doesn't find me attractive or interesting anymore."**

What would she have felt?

- ♦ **Anger**
- ♦ **Resentment**
- ♦ **Grief**
- ♦ **Self-pity**

98

Maybe she should have been more probing; or given more time to her husband. Did she know her husband well enough to arrive at these conclusions?

In fact Roger must have been having a tough time at work. A bad review by the boss, a fall in profits in business, tiff with a colleague. It could have been anything!

The point is nothing in life has any meaning, only the meaning you give it.

Roger must have had a completely unconnected problem, but to Lynette it looked like a problem in their relationship!

Controlling your inner voice and what you say to yourself either makes or breaks your self-esteem and confidence.

Within this session, you will be introduced to a technique, which you can use to control your inner dialogue and to make you appraise just how hard and unreasonable you are on yourself.

But before we get into the exercise, let's just discuss those negative thoughts you have.

Here's a small little recap – *It is not the trigger or the event that instigates the bad feelings. But the internal dialogues you say to yourself in response to the trigger that makes you despondent.*

Okay, to make it easier to understand, let's split these negative thoughts or distortions into 13 categories.

Here's the list. You can use this as a quick reference:

1. **Assuming**

2. **Over-generalising**

3. **'Shoulds'**

4. **Labelling**

5. **Binning the positives**

6. **And they all lived happily ever after**

7.   Blaming other people and events

8.   It's all or nothing!

9.   Negative thinking erodes your soul!

10. Believing what you feel

11. Personalizing

12. Making comparisons with others

13. I can't cope with life

While we go through them one by one, make notes of the ones you use most frequently.

1.   Assuming

When you make assumptions with your thinking, you are assuming the worst without knowing the full picture or without testing the evidence.

Let's go back to our example about Lynette and her husband. She didn't have any of the facts; she just assumed that her relationship with her husband was in deep trouble.

She could have tested the assumption by going up to him and saying "Roger, did I do something that upset you? What's wrong? I think we should talk this out." Other examples of assuming self-talk are:

- **"I know this project is going to be rubbish"**
- **"I know I'll make loads of mistakes if I'm best man"**
- **"I know people will just hate me"**

How could you rephrase some of these thoughts above to make them more realistic? Example – "I am going to give this project a chance and make up my own mind."

2.   Over-generalising

This is when you over-generalize your thoughts and make them more intense by the words you use.

For instance, you would say things like:

- **"I always end up on the losing side."**
- **"I make mistakes in everything I do."**
- **"Everyone hates me."**
- **"Everyone thinks I am so dumb."**
- **"I never do any good at cooking."**

Even when you read these lines their demoralizing effect is so evident!

As much as you know that such over-generalizing internal dialogues are inaccurate, unjust and unfair and affect your confidence, yet you use them.

You certainly are not making mistakes in everything you do?!

C'mon! You think you are making a mistake right now?

Rubbish! It's not everything that you do then, is it?

How do you turn this around?

Well, a better phrase to use would be, "Sometimes my cooking doesn't turn out very well but overall I am a good cook."

Sounds fair?

Look for the good in situations and what is working well. It can do wonders!

3.   'Shoulds'

Some people surround themselves with 'Shoulds'.

- **"I should be thinner."**
- **"I should have more friends."**
- **"I should be earning more money."**

Are you the kind who says 'should' all the time?

'Shoulds' are the demands you place on yourself.

A 'should' represents what you are not doing but you think you should be!

So when you know you 'should' be doing something but are not doing it, how do you feel?

Inadequate, hopeless, frustrated? Yes, the list can go on. So, what are your plans to get rid of the 'shoulds'?

It's easy. Just change the 'should' to 'want' or 'could'.

♦ **"I want to do this"**
♦ **"How could I do this?"**

4. Labelling

How often do you use an adjective to describe yourself?

Labelling is a common syndrome. This is when you give yourself a name or statement that describes who you are.

For example:

♦ **"I am a loser."**
♦ **"I am stupid."**
♦ **"I am ugly."**
♦ **"I am fat."**

How is it possible that you are a loser in every aspect of your life? Is there nothing in you that is attractive? Are you forever a dimwit?

Of course not!

Stop labelling yourself and be specific in your thoughts.

Instead of saying "I am a loser" say "That didn't work out how I would have liked."

5.   Binning the positives

Do you tend to overlook the compliments people give you?

Do you refuse to accept and ignore if someone says "That was a great job, well done" or "You look fantastic today"?

How do you usually reply to praise?

"Oh, it was nothing, it was easy" or "I don't look great really, you're just saying that."

Do you realize that you've just discounted the fact that you worked really hard to get that job done or that you take time over your appearance to get it right?

Let's set this record straight. A simple "Thank you" with a smile is the perfect response.

Think it over. Is it that much of an effort?

You would give credit to someone who did a great job. Make sure you accept the credit when you do a great job or when you receive a compliment.

6.   And they all lived happily ever after

Perfection is an illusion.

Oh yes it is. No point arguing here.

So if you are a person who has to have everything perfect in your life, it's going to be pretty tough, buddy! You are setting yourself up for disappointments.

Do you have thoughts like:

- ◆   **"That shouldn't happen to me."**
- ◆   **"I can't believe that has happened."**
- ◆   **"That's unfair."**

Stop looking for that perfect world. Everyone has things happen to him or her, good and bad. You are not a special case and no one is exempt.

Instead accept that bad times fall on all and ask yourself "What could I do to improve this situation now?"

7. Blaming other people and events

Do you blame others and don't accept responsibility for outcomes that are different from your expectations?

Do you say:

- ◆ **"If only my parents had been more ambitious I'd have had more success by now."**
- ◆ **"If only I didn't have to impress all of the time."**
- ◆ **"He make's me feel so bad."**
- ◆ **"She had a hold over me which means I can't do anything."**

While this attitude is awful, it will also make you feel like a 'victim'. Forever you will move ahead with a sense of helplessness; that you are capable of nothing.

It isn't your fault. Is it?

YES, IT IS!

Agreed, the event has had an effect on you but at the end of the day only you have the responsibility to let it affect you.

So, how do you turn these thoughts around?

Well, for starters, focus on the reality.

If you feel something is unfair or unjust, accept that it is.

Then accept that the impact it has on you is your responsibility.

Don't make excuses; it is your responsibility!

8. It's all or nothing!

There's more than just black and white. There are several colors in between, right? Like blue, green, red, yellow, pink, brown, purple, mauve...phew!

Then why are most aspects of life just black or white? Are you one of those who think "It's all or nothing"?

Is there no grey area in between?!

- "I am either a success or a failure."
- "If I get first place, I am a winner. If I get second place, I am a loser", irrespective if there are 20,000 runners!
- "If I don't get things 100% perfect I am a flop."
- "If I don't get an A Grade in Math, I am a failure."

Well, in life there are rarely successes and failures. In fact, success is a journey, not a destination.

Success and failure are not meant to be measured on a 100 or 0 scale. At the end of the day if you don't perform to your highest standards, it certainly doesn't mean you scored a zero!

Your "It's all or nothing" thought is only setting you up for failures.

How many times do you perform with absolute perfection?

Less than 10% of the time!

So, does that mean you are a failure 90% of the time?

Now you know that's utter nonsense.

Why so you always have to be perfect?

9. Negative thinking erodes your soul!

How do you react to events that don't work out the way you planned?

Negatively?

For instance, your boss has said that you completed a piece of work incorrectly, so you say to your partner that you have had a terrible day.

You may have burnt the pie, so the whole meal is ruined.

You might have cut your finger while hiking so the entire holiday is messed up.

Your thought makes the entire situation negative.

What happens if you change your focus when you start thinking negatively?

You can say:

- ♦ **"What is still good about this situation?"**
- ♦ **"That is only one bad thing, what are the good things?"**
- ♦ **"What could I still enjoy about this experience?"**

10. Believing what you feel

Feelings are not facts. If you believe your feelings blindly, just too bad, my friend. Mend your ways or you are sure to suffer a confidence setback.

The quality of your life is based upon the quality of your feelings.

Feelings are only thoughts that we have decided to generate. That doesn't make them real.

You give meaning to your thoughts; and hence your feelings.

So, are you the type of person who believes all the feelings you have?

- ♦ **"I feel bad. Therefore, I must be bad."**
- ♦ **"I feel like a loser. Therefore, I must be a loser."**
- ♦ **"I feel ugly. Therefore, I must be ugly."**

Low levels of confidence can distort your thoughts. So you really need to question your feelings before you believe them.

Ask yourself questions like:

- ♦ **"What would someone who is a 100% loser, is bad or ugly be like?"**
- ♦ **"Am I really like that?"**

Challenge your feelings by questioning them.

11. Personalizing

Personalizing is when you blame yourself.

Personalizing happens when you say:

- ♦ **"It's entirely my fault that my son didn't get the chances in life."**
- ♦ **"If I wasn't so clingy, men would stay with me."**
- ♦ **"It's all my fault that we got divorced."**

Blaming yourself for other's actions and decision means you are taking too many responsibilities on your shoulders.

Don't!

Simply because you are not accountable for someone else's decision-making.

Remember that you are not the only one giving advice or offering opinions. An individual meets numerous people and hence gets a number of opinions. But in the end he or she has the freedom to decide what he or she wants to do.

Agreed mistakes do happen and some of them could be the result of your action or decision. But all of them?! You don't believe that, do you?

Your confidence is suffering a blow every time you hold yourself liable for someone else's life turning out to be miserable.

Take the reigns of your life into your hands. Don't blame yourself and don't let others do it unjustly.

12. Making comparisons with others

Do you always compare yourself to others?

If you do, it's high time you stop.

Why are you putting yourself through so much of worthless competition? Frankly, it isn't even healthy competition.

What you are doing through such a comparison is magnify your 'weaknesses' and others' 'strengths' or shrink others' 'weaknesses' and your 'strengths'.

So, are you saying something like this?

- **"I haven't got a chance for this job, after all who is going to want to hire a single Mum? Maria is young, single and she has got a degree."**
- **"I am hopeless at spelling and math, Mark is great at these, he can do them standing on his head."**
- **"No-one will want to go out with me, I've got a big nose. Look at Donna. She is beautiful, has lovely hair and really nice skin."**

Challenge these thoughts!

Appreciate that you are a unique person and stop these distortions.

13. I can't cope with life

If you find yourself saying stuff like:

- **"I can't stand it."**
- **"I couldn't live without you."**
- **"I can manage this."**

So what are you doing? Accepting defeat and telling yourself that you are not strong enough to cope with life?

Yes, a lot of things in life are unpleasant, difficult and not nice.

But you can cope with it!

A better way of saying something is:

- **"I don't really like this but I can stand it."**

How do you challenge and question this thinking? By asking the following:

- ♦ **"If this does happen, will I really be helpless and be unable to cope?"**
- ♦ **"If the worst happens, what will I do?"**
- ♦ **"When I look back in 30 years time, will anyone really care about this?"**

2 – 4

How To Overcome Negative Comments From Others

Nothing has any meaning in life, only the meaning you give to it.

You've heard that before, haven't you? How far have you come to believe in it?

It's not what people say to you that is a problem. People talk! Yes, they do, and there is nothing you can do to stop them. However, it's what you say to yourself after people say something unpleasant that leads to a problem.

Are you left behind with a feeling of dejection?

Let's tackle that feeling, and banish it from our lives!

How to respond to confidence destroyers

Like we discussed a few seconds ago that people talk and it's hardly possible to stop them. In such a case, how do you respond to negative comments coming from others with or without an intention to make you feel miserable about yourself?

For instance, when Candace wore a new bold pink dress to office, her colleague Syrah said, "Yikes! That's way too bright Candace." With her nose up in the air, Syrah ranted on, "I would never wear something like that."

What do you think Candace would have said?

"Eh... Yea... I did think it was too bright. Maybe I shouldn't have worn it. Why did I even buy it?"

But Candace did not sulk or curse herself. In fact, this is what she said, and please note, with a twinkle in her eyes☺ :

"I know Syrah, this color is really bold. But you know what; it makes me feel bright and happy. Maybe I could spread some of my vivacity to others around me. What say you?"

You bet Syrah was quite taken aback. And you know what, a couple of weeks later, she might have bought herself a dress the same color!

Candace didn't stop wearing bright-colored clothes. She could carry them off and was comfortable in depicting a vibrant personality. She believed in what she did.

Doesn't this incident agree with the fact – No one can make you feel inferior without your consent?

It's not what people say to you that affects your confidence. It's what you say to yourself after they've stopped talking that either makes or breaks your self esteem.

Every feeling tells you something, but you should learn to take them with a pinch of salt.

Remember it has been made up by what you have been thinking and saying to yourself.

It will take time to learn them all, but build up gradually and you will start to build up your confidence.

Here are a few feelings and thoughts that you are sure to face sometime or the other. Check what kind of action you can practice in such a case.

FEELING: "I don't feel confident about the way I look"

ACTION: Improve your overall appearance. Would losing or putting on (in case you are painfully thin) some weight make you feel great? If so DO IT! What clothes would your Confidence Role Model wear to feel good? Get a new haircut and treat yourself to some new clothes – it always makes you feel better and more confident. Buy something new each month and when you put it on, view it as your own confidence booster.

FEELING: "I'm afraid of that person – I'm never confident around him/her"

ACTION: Just remember, they eat, sleep, go to the toilet just like you do and mostly they have the same problems as you - they just don't show it! Think – How would your Confidence Role Model deal with this person? What would they do?

Remember that confidence is about acting – they are just better actors than you right now. Think of the things you can do that they can't do – how would they feel if the roles were reversed? Getting any closer?

FEELING: "I'm afraid of the feedback and reaction I'm going to get when I complete this piece of work"

ACTION: Hey, as long as you've done everything to the best of your ability, you don't have to worry. And if you do make a mistake or two, what the heck?! Just learn from them for next time. A person who never makes mistakes is not doing anything. Those people who moan and groan about things always seem to do nothing. There are no failures in life as long as you learn from the outcome. You're a winner!

FEELING: "I'm really worried about this..."

ACTION: Time to usher in your Confidence Role Model again (when did you ever let her/him go, right?). Would my Confidence Role Model worry about this? How would they deal with this situation? What would they do? In the grand scheme of things what will worrying do to this problem? Is there any action I can take to fix this right now?

FEELING: "My friends are really negative thinkers and this just festers onto me when I'm with them"

ACTION: Don't get rid of your friends but make sure you surround yourself with positive and progressive people also. Surround yourself with people who are like your role model.

You know what your friends are like beforehand, so just accept them for what they are. If they are true friends just acknowledge that they are who they are and you are who you are.

FEELING: "I can't do this"

ACTION: Oh yes you can! Break the problem down into small chunks and attack each chunk separately. Nothing is ever as daunting as it first seems. How would your Confidence Role Model do this? Think of a time where you have done something really difficult – think this through in your mind and play it over and over like a video recording before you do the task in hand.

FEELING: "I've never got enough money to do the things that I want"

ACTION: Ask yourself what you are doing about it? Do you have the "more month left at the end of the money" rather that "more money left at the end of the month" problem? Do you plan your budget? Do you know where all your money goes? If you answered yes to the first question and no to the next two, it's time you made a plan of action. For all you know, you may need another career to achieve the lifestyle you want?

FEELING: "I don't feel worthwhile as a person"

ACTION: Put down your strengths on a piece of paper. Don't forget to list down all your achievements in life from your exams, to when you passed your driving test, to the job interviews you cleared etc. Remind yourself that you've already had loads of successes and don't feel so sorry for yourself. After all, no matter where you are in life, there is always someone who is worse off than you. Put things into perspective; ask yourself what your Role Model would do.

More Actions

We are not done yet, so pick up a fresh piece of paper.

Write down all of those confidence destroying statements that you say to yourself or others say to you.

Now, write down what you are going to replace these thoughts with after the statements are made.

Write down next to each statement, why it is downright twaddle.

Confidence sapping friends & colleagues

The people whom you hang out with, that is, family, friends or colleagues, they will have either a positive or negative affect on your levels of self-esteem and confidence.

You are sure to have been around people who are positive, happy and pleasant.

They are the ones who make you feel a welcome sight any day, who smile sincerely, and who encourage you rather than rain you down with advices and reprieves.

How do they make you feel?

Their personality rubs on to you too, making you feel positive, happy and pleasant. Such lively people can easily sprinkle zest into a boring atmosphere and can fill a room with constructive energy and upbeat vibes.

You must be familiar with the moaners too.

They are always putting people down, they don't like others being successful, they are jealous and are negative thinkers. Phew! That's a long list and it sure can go on.

Such people bleed dry your energy, bring down your energy levels and in a way take you a million miles away from the level you really want to be operating on. They try and urge you to join their team – a team of non-achievers.

Family members can be grumblers a lot of times, but you can always choose your friends; you can never choose your family!

So what should you do to make sure that the people you hang out with empower and support what you stand for rather than bring you down all of the time?

1. You have the power to choose who you hang out with. Ideally, you want happy, vibrant and positive people. Say, people who are more like Candace and less like Syrah.

2. If you have good friends who are negative and yet you want to hang around them, make a point of letting them know how you feel - if they are true friends, they will respect you for this. If they are negative from time to time, just acknowledge that this is what they are like and block out the negativity.

3. The same can be applied to family. Your more mature family members have behaviours that have been conditioned for years. Appreciate where they have come from and stated before, select and elicit the information that filters through to your brain.

4. And remember to keep this statement in your minds always – Nothing has meaning in life except the meaning you give it.

2 – 5

How To Feel Confident All The Time

Self-confidence is essential..

The power of the mind is truly remarkable

How you feel in any given moment is linked to:

- ♦ **What you are focusing on**
- ♦ **The way you are moving and using your body**
- ♦ **The language you are using**

No doubt, your mind controls all three.

The moment you feel lethargic or need an instant confidence/ energy boost just change the way you feel by changing the above 3 points.

1. What you are focusing on

Stay conscious of what you are focusing on in that particular moment.

Are they negative and lethargic thoughts? Low in confidence? Are they indicating that you would fail? Are you telling yourself that you feel low in energy?

Yes?

What would you have to focus on to feel vibrant and full of energy? What should you focus on to feel confident?

On the other hand, if you are feeling vibrant and energized right now, what are you thinking about?

2. The way you are moving and using your body

This is also called your physiology.

Emotion is created by motion, and the fewer movements you make the less energy you will have!

Moreover, the type of movements you make either pump you up or make you languid and want to doze off.

Observe your body when you are feeling low in confidence.

Are you sitting down? Is your head up or down? Are your shoulders slouched? Are you walking slowly or quickly? Are your facial muscles moving? What are you doing with your hands?

Write down all the characteristics of a confident person. Imagine there is a confident person before you now. How would they be moving their body?

It's your turn to feel energized and confident. Ready?

Okay!

Copy the movements that you just wrote down when you are feeling low and, WHOA! You'll become confident!

3. The language you are using

The words you say to yourself both in your mind and out aloud will have an impact on how you are feeling.

What words do you use to describe negative emotions?

Do you say? :

"I'm feeling tired"

"I'm stupid"

"I'm angry"

"I'm livid"

"I'm overwhelmed"

 "I'm depressed"

Write down some more common phrases like those above that you use:

The intensity of those negative sayings will have an effect on how you feel and whether you feel confident or not.

What if instead of – **"I'm really nervous"**, you said to yourself – **"I'm really excited"**?

Would it make you feel better?

Of course it would.

The feelings and emotions linked to nervousness and excitement are actually the same. It's just that you are giving the adrenaline right direction.

So, what other words could you replace the negative sayings with?

Try swapping:

"I'm feeling tired" to **"I'm feeling unresourceful"**

"I'm stupid" to **"I'm learning"**

"I'm angry" to **"I'm a little annoyed"**

"I'm livid" to **"I'm a little miffed"**

"I'm overwhelmed" to **"I'm feeling busy"**

"I'm feeling insecure" to **"I'm questioning"**

"I'm depressed" to **"I'm not on top of things"**

As the intensity of the words lower, the intensity of the feelings lessen too.

Let's move on with some simple exercises.

Write down 5 old negative sayings or phrases that you say on a consistent basis and replace them with new empowering and less intensified ones:

Just as you lower the intensity of words to lessen negative feelings, you can apply the reverse to feel magnificent and confident every single day!

Change your vocabulary to improve the quality of your day.

How?

Increase the intensity; increase the feeling when you use positive/good words.

Want an example? Here you go...

Instead of saying **"I feel good,"** say **"I feel fantastic!"**

It's as simple as that.

Here are some more:

Change:

"I feel ok" to **"I feel awesome"**

"I feel motivated" to **"I am driven"**

"I feel confident" to **"I feel unstoppable"**

"I feel energized" to **"I feel juiced"**

Change the "good" words of the present to "magnificent" words of the future.

When you implement this, the impact will be AWESOME!

How To Lead A Confident Life

Congratulations!

You have finally reached the last session of this Confidence Building course!

We hope by now you are more of a DOER than just a READER.

With this course you will get going only if you put into action all that you picked up. Reading alone will be of no good.

Your confidence will shoot high only if you are a doer, and on that note let's kick off the last session.

****
The New Confident You!
****

Are you all pumped up with confidence as you reach the final stages of this course?

Have you been putting into action all those recommendations that you came across in this course?

If yes, we are glad that you are really serious about making a difference to your life by increasing your confidence levels and self-esteem. **Good Going!**

Trust that you are prepared to do an analysis of how you felt before and how you feel now.

Compare by writing them down as this will help you clarify everything and make them official.

We understand this could be difficult, arranging the thoughts without being subjective. But you bet you will feel great once you are done. At least, relieved!

And you know what? If you have done this smoothly, you are already a champion.

Yes! You heard it right! CHAMPION! And you now have that self-confidence you always wanted.

You have taken the first step and you deserve to treat yourself. Go out and watch a movie, or dine in a posh restaurant, or get yourself a new dress.

While you treat yourself, don't forget to take note of how your confidence has been building over the past 6 weeks.

Jot down all the things you have noticed that illustrate that your confidence is improving, no matter how small or large they are.

We will now give you an **8-point reminder** that will perform as a quick reference on how to get confidence in any given situation.

1. **Think through your desired outcome - Ask yourself – "How would a person with confidence do this?"**

2. **Visualize yourself doing the tasks. Close your eyes and see yourself doing it successfully.**

3. **Prepare thoroughly. What are you going to say? How are you going to say it?**

4. **Before you do it, go through it in your mind several times and be positive.**

5. **Put it into perspective - No matter what it is, in 50 years' time will people really care about it?**

6. **DO IT!**

7. **Learn from the outcome you get for next time.**

8. **REWARD yourself for DOING rather than TALKING about doing it!**

****
****

Well, here you are, all confident and ready to face the world as this module comes to an end.

Hope you have gained enough from this course to last you a lifetime because remember, you only live once and hence you have to make the most of every opportunity and every moment that comes your way.

And every time someone tries to give a blow to your confidence, just think what David Brinkley said:

A successful person is one who can lay a firm foundation with the bricks that others throw at him or her

All the best for a BRIGHT & CONFIDENT future

Section 3
Effective Communication Skills

How to get what you want through effective communication

Introduction

A partner of a leading firm comes back to his office and says to his manager, *"Did you get my message where I said, 'Ship the Enron documents to the Feds?'"* The manager goes white. *"Oh My God! I thought you said rip the Enron documents to shreds!"*

That's what happens when there is an error in communication. How can you make sure it never happens?

Communication is without doubt the most important skill required to live successfully. The world around you is competitive to say the least. Whether at home or at the workplace, at a mall, or with friends, if you can communicate well, you have got most things going your way. People do not just listen to a good communicator; they are ready to bend or unbend to the person's needs.

Not everybody is privileged to gain communication skills from the word 'go'. However, all one needs is a goal to become a successful communicator and find the right source to pick up the skills, half the job is done.

One such source from where you can pick up communication skills from scratch or refine those you already have is this "Effective Communication Skills" e-course.

This section is divided into 6 modules inclusive of exercises and assignments that will teach you the essence of effective communication and enable you to express yourself more clearly and confidently. Moreover, the modules are simple and going through this course will be smooth-sailing.

Now go ahead, and COMMUNICATE!

3 - 1

Understanding The Communications Process – How Does Miscommunication Occur?

Communication is vital to all of us, for without this skill we will be quite helpless and the world around us would be blank. After all every person, be it a worker, manager or a teenager, have interactions with other people almost all throughout their life.

It is easy to tell a person to do a task but the person may not interpret your command properly, thus resulting in a task that may not match your exact requirements.

That is where the difference between communicating and communicating effectively becomes apparent.

Always remember that an effective communication goes far beyond the words you say. For a communication process to be effective, one has to know the other person's views and the style of absorbing information.

In short, if you want to convey your message across to the other persons' mind, you need to adopt a style and approach that will evoke the desired response.

Effective communicators are well versed in the action signals and communication strategies that can be brought out from a person and adopt their style to make sure that their communications are effective.

In this chapter we will cover the basic process of communication and the issues that lead to miscommunication.

Before we go ahead, how about we do an exercise? After all it is practice that makes one perfect.

Take a blank piece of paper and write your name in the middle and then around your name write down the names of people with whom you have frequent communication or communication. This list will include friends, family, work colleagues, etc.

As you work through this course keep referring back to this diagram of the people whom you interact with the most and apply what you learn from them as individuals. Effective communication is all about tailoring your communication strategy for different people. NO TWO PEOPLE ARE ALIKE!

The Communication Process

The Communications Process

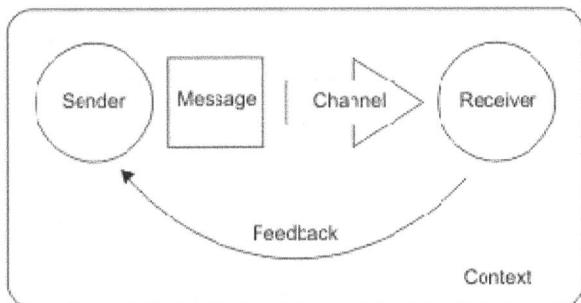

The purpose of communication is to get your message across to others. This is a process that involves exchanging information between a sender and a receiver. Communication is the process of exchanging information through a common system of symbols, signs, behavior, speech, writing and signals.

Let us analyze how this exchange works.

To start the exchange we need a sender who has information that needs to be conveyed and then we need a receiver who is to accept this information.

Now the sender prepares the information in an organized manner and passes it to the receiver through a proper channel (text, speech etc).

So that's how easy it is! Just think, arrange and express!

Easy it is but the process leaves room for error, often causing unnecessary confusion and counter productivity between the sender and the receiver.

Say, for instance the case of an employee you heard "You are fired!!" instead of "You are hired!!"

Let's consider the incident we mentioned at the beginning of this course- the business partner and his manager. The conversation was a very simple one but because of certain discrepancies ending up with disastrous consequences. So where did it all go haywire?

In that particular episode, the partner (sender) wanted the documents shipped to the feds (information). Now according to the definition the sender has arranged his information in an organized manner and passed it onto the receiver (the manager). Now the receiver seems to have got the message but he had a rather distorted interpretation of the message.

Let us bring up the partner and his thought process that lead to this conversation.

He thinks of the idea "ship the documents to Feds" then he represents this thought in form words or text and expresses it through speech.

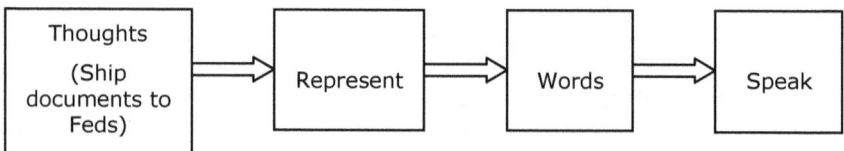

Thoughts (Ship documents to Feds)	→	Represent	→	Words	→	Speak

Well so far so good.

Enter the manager into this conversation and unfortunately the communication leads to a disaster!

The manager receives the message and he interprets ship as rip and fed as shred! And comprehends the message as "Rip the documents to shreds".

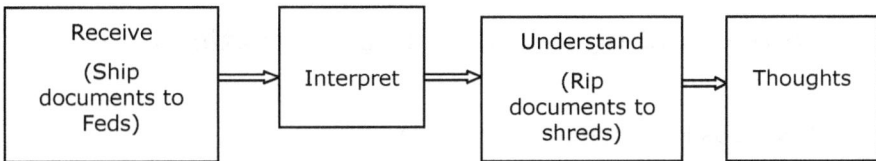

Receive (Ship documents to Feds)	Interpret	Understand (Rip documents to shreds)	Thoughts

Here the information underwent a total change during the receiver's interpretation.

This misunderstanding of information could have happened due to the internal filter system of the person or the environment in which the information exchanges took place.

Now what is an internal filter? The name may sound new but internal filters are a vital system for every one of us.

The internal filter within each person decides the way we look at the world. These filters are basically sensory input channels like visual system, auditory system and kinesthetic system.

Here's an idea of what these input channels do:

Visual system helps us study and analyze the body language and physiology of others.

Auditory system enables us to hear the words spoken and the tones in which others speak.

Kinesthetic system is split into internal and external feelings. Internal feelings include feelings like hunger, stress, tension, comfort, pleasure etc. External feelings include touching someone or something, what it feels like – texture, pressure etc.

Based on our experiences, the filters create internal, mental maps of reality. When we communicate, whether through gestures and actions or verbally through language, we do so, based on our mental maps.

The information we get is received by the filters and gets coupled with our emotional state and this determines our reactions.

Now let us see how the filters influence our understanding of a message and our reactions.

Understanding information and reactions

Now let us look at another example:

Cary Grant is said to have been reluctant to reveal his age to the public, having played the youthful lover for more years than would have been appropriate. One day, while he was sorting out some business with his agent, a telegram arrived from a journalist who was desperate to learn how old the actor was. It read:

HOW OLD CARY GRANT?

Grant, who happened to open it himself, immediately cabled back:

OLD CARY GRANT FINE. HOW YOU?

What do you analyze from this example?

It looks like Cary Grant got the message clearly but he deduced the question's purpose and answered it in a totally different manner.

Now how did that happen?

When we get information, it is analyzed and modified in our mind in relation to the ideas and thoughts that linger in our mind. So when a person receives a message, he/she interprets the message in their preferred wording and language.

Our understanding is mainly influenced by a certain filters, to be precise, 6 filters.

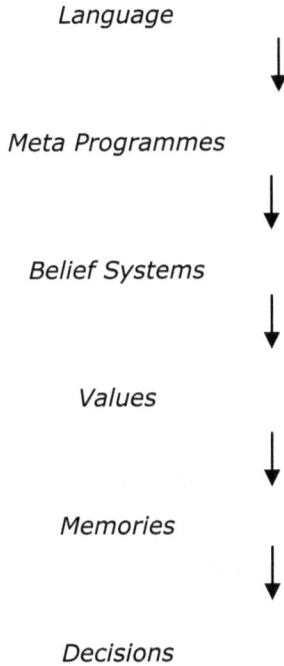

Language

↓

Meta Programmes

↓

Belief Systems

↓

Values

↓

Memories

↓

Decisions

Now let us take a deeper look into these filters that run our think tank!

Language

Language helps us recognize words depending on whether we understand them in the first place and our previous experience of using them.

Our usage and understanding of words will be decisive in interpreting a message.

For example, the term "How old Cary Grant?" was a journalist's query about Cary Grant's age but the latter understood the message as a query about his health.

Meta programmes

Most of us tend to assume everyone is just like we are and we communicate with others the way we want information to be delivered to us. The problem is that everyone doesn't think the way we do and look at things the way we perceive them.

Meta programs are a set of thought and behavior patterns that operate beyond the conscious level. These patterns control one's attention during conversation, habitual linguistic patterns and body language, and so on.

Knowing a person's Meta programmes will help you to predict their behavior and actions a lot better.

Since this aspect will help one to communicate specifically in the way an individual needs to receive information. I have dedicated a chapter entirely for this aspect.

Values

Values have a great impact on our motivation.

They shape the way we address people, how we work, listen and evaluate information. They differentiate what is important and what is good or bad for us.

Beliefs

Beliefs correspond to reality and are mostly derived from valid evidence and arguments. Beliefs are the presupposition that we have about the world and things around us.

During a communication it is important to know ones' beliefs as many of the views that come up during a conversation is based on certain sets of beliefs and preconceived notions.

After all, you do not want to talk about Hitler's ideas and his book when conversing about literature with a Jewish friend.

Memories

This filter is all about our recollection of past events.

Memory plays a very important role in human communication. It helps to maintain the thread of a conversation; it ensures that topics are fully discussed.

Moreover, experiences help us react and give feedbacks, whether negative or positive, to certain topics during a conversation.

For example if a budding tennis player was to ask Pete Sampras, "What is so great about Wimbledon?", Sampras would be pleased and would be very happy to share his experiences.

If the youngster asks him about The French Open, Sampras will probably say "It is tough to play in French Open; clay surface is not as comfortable as grass surface."

Here Sampras, a record seven time winner at Wimbledon and French Open struggler, would always have rather bad memories of the French Open, while Wimbledon will always be cherished by him.

Decisions

This is the final filter and is linked closely to memories.

If we have made some good, bad or indifferent decisions in the past we may have created some empowering or disempowering beliefs either about the decision itself or the outcome.

For example, if a woman has had a particularly bad relationship with a man she may say that "All men are the same" and never want to get into a relationship for a long time.

A decision taken by us is expressed in our action and body language.

How Miscommunication Occurs

Once information has been analyzed through our filters, there will be a distortion of information due to deletion as we only pay attention to certain aspects of the information that can be linked to our experiences.

This leads to misrepresentations of the information and an unexpected feedback thus resulting in a miscommunication

Most of us generalize information when we draw conclusions that may be sufficiently different for other people to misunderstand.

If we look at the earlier mentioned example of the woman, we see she has generalized all men as bad at maintaining a good relationship. This is obviously not the case with all men, for if it was, then the world would be one hostile place to live in.

I think it is time we wrap up this chapter.

Before we go into the next chapter, Let us do a recap of what we have learned and refresh our memory with a few exercises.

⊥ **We receive information via one of our senses.**

⊥ **Our filters then determine our internal representation of that event.**

- It is our internal representation that puts us in a certain state and this in turns creates our physiology.

- The state in which we find ourselves, will determine our behavior or reaction to what happens around us.

Exercises

Appreciating Your Own Values and Those Of Others

Write down all the values and beliefs you have.

For example, what things that you want to experience and have? Success? Freedom? Adventure? Security?

Then, write a list of the things you want to avoid? Rejection? Pain? Failure? Boredom?

Now, have a look at your list and do the same thing for the people who you communicate to the most.

Are you the same? Where do you differ? Build up a mental picture of how they see the world.

This is where we end our first session, hope you got some direction and will continue benefiting from our proceeding sessions.

How To Understand Someone's View Of The World

Hello and welcome to the second part of the Effective Communication module.

In this module and the next we are going to look into how people think the way they do and how you should tailor your communication style to meet their view of the world.

Meta Programmes

Just so you can refresh your memory from the previous chapter – Meta Programmes are an internal filter that we pass information through.

They are specifically related to the way that we sort and categorize information.

Meta programmes go a long way in predicting someone's actions. However, please note that there are no right or wrong Meta programmes.

There are several Meta programmes but let's go through the top 6 that are used in everyday and business contexts:

- ♦ **Towards/Away from**
- ♦ **Frame of Reference**

- **Sameness/Difference**
- **Reason**
- **Chunk Size**
- **Convincer**

Towards/away

'Towards people' always strive to achieve an outcome. They want to move towards something.

In their move towards a certain outcome or goal they find it difficult to recognize what should be avoided. Instead they concentrate and focus on what they will get when the outcome is achieved.

On the other hand, 'Away from' people are in an effort to avoid a certain situation. They don't want to experience loss or discomfort and want to move away from something.

Now then, what do you do if you want to know what type of person is someone?

Simple!

Ask them this type of a question:

What do you want? What will having 'xyz' give you? What do you want in 'xyz'?

This is what their response will tell you:

'Toward' people will tell you what they want.

'Away from' people will tell you what they don't want.

Now comes the questions as in how to communicate with people who have a 'Towards' or an 'Away from' strategy.

This is what you do when in *negotiations* with such people:

'Towards'

Work out what their goals are and what you can do to help them achieve these goals. Focus on the outcome and what it will give them.

'Away from'

Work out what you can do to help them avoid what they don't want. Work out and anticipate potential problems and assure them that these can be minimized or avoided.

You can *manage* such people in this fashion:

'Towards'

Offer incentives, i.e. an outcome. Emphasize their goals and what and how they can achieve them.

'Away from'

Use sanctions. Be aware that these people are usually the ones to bring up problems.

Influencing Language

'Towards'

Get, achieve, attain, include, obtain, have, want etc.

'Away from'

Not have, avoid, don't want, keep away from, get rid of etc.

FRAME OF REFERENCE

The second major Meta programme is your frame of reference.

This is all about how people evaluate things and can be split out into two:

- Internal People
- External People

Internal People stand true to their opinion and evaluate on the basis of what they think is appropriate. They make all decisions themselves and can have difficulty in accepting other people's feedback and direction.

External People, on the other hand, evaluate on the basis of what other people think is appropriate. They need others to guide, direct and motivate them. Since they cannot decide for themselves, they need external references.

So, how do you know if someone is an Internal or an External person?

Ask them this type of question:

How do you know that you have done a good job? How do you know that?

And their response will speak for itself.

Internal people will tell you that they decide when they've done a good job.

External people tell you that they know because other people or outside information sources tell them.

Now when you are in *negotiations* with these people, this is what you should do:

Internal

Emphasize to the person that they will know inside that they are right. Say that they have to decide. Don't bother about external factors or what other people think, they will not be interested in this.

External

Emphasize what others think. Give them data and information to back things up. Give them feedback and reassurance.

Manage these people like this:

Internal

These people have difficulty in accepted feedback or praise. They like to decide for themselves and don't like to be told what to do. They do best when they have little or no supervision. So, just let them be. Don't try to force your opinion down their throat.

External

These people need close management. They need constant feedback and re-assurance about how well they are doing. They need to be told what to do, how to do it and how well they are doing it. Be supportive and encouraging to them.

Influencing language

Internal

You know best, you'll know when it's right, only you can decide, it's up to you etc.

External

Can I give you some feedback, I will let you know, the facts show, other people think that etc.

SAMENESS/DIFFERENCE

This Meta programme is all about people's perceptions of likeness and differences.

There are 4 main categories with this:

'Sameness' people will notice those things that are the same or match their previous experiences. They dislike change.

'Sameness with exception' people will first notice the similarities and will then notice the differences. They prefer slow or gradual change.

'Difference with exception' people will notice the differences and then the similarities. They like change and variety.

'Difference' people will notice those things that are different. They love change and want it all of the time.

So, how do you know what type of person they are?

Time to ask them this type of question:

What is the relationship between these three objects? What is the relationship between this X and a previous Y?

What their response will tell you:

'Sameness' people will tell you what similar qualities the objects have.

'Sameness with exception' people will tell you first how things are similar and then tell you what differences they have.

'Difference with exception' people will tell you first how things are different and then give you the similarities.

'Difference' people will plainly tell you what the differences are.

You can use this in the real world in the following manner:

In *negotiations* with these people:

'Sameness'

Stress areas of agreement. Do not discuss differences. Discuss areas of similarities, how you both want the same thing.

'Sameness with exception'

First stress similarities and then point out the differences. Talk about change as a gradual slow process.

'Difference with exception'

First stress how things are different and only then talk about similarities. Focus on change and new solutions

'Difference'

Stress how things are totally different. Do not mention similarities. Talk in terms of massive change and revolutionary.

In *managing* these people:

'Sameness'

Have them do things the same way. They hate variety so don't talk about it. Instead, talk about continuity.

'Sameness with exception'

Have them do the same things but with gradual improvements and changes. Initiate a gradual process of change by talking about it.

'Difference with exception'

Downplay commonality by emphasizing improvements and changes. Stress different ways to do the job and make changes frequently.

'Difference'

Talk about the differences. These people will get bored at repetitive tasks. So have them do something new all the time

Influencing language

'Sameness'

Same, same as, maintain, keep doing, in common, keep the same, usual, similar etc.

'Sameness with exception'

Better, more, less, gradual, although, but, same except etc.

'Difference with exception'

Different, new, changed, change, unusual etc.

'Difference'

Different, new, radical, unique, revolutionary etc.

REASON

The Meta programme called Reason is all about people's opinions towards making choices, developing options and following procedures.

Here, there are two types of people:

- ◆ 'Options'
- ◆ 'Procedures'

'Options' People are very good at developing choices. They want to experiment and therefore are more of rule breakers or benders than rule followers. They are very good at making improvements and developing new procedures or alternatives to old ones.

'Procedures' people are good at following procedures, and thus, are rule followers. But they do not know how to generate them. When they have not got a procedure to follow, they get stuck.

So, here's the question – How do you know what type of a particular person is?

Answer – Ask them this type of question:

Why did you choose xyz?

Their response will tell you:

'Options' people will give you the reasons why they did it.

'Procedures' people will tell you a story about how they came to do what they did. They don't talk about choices or options. They give you the impression that they don't have choices.

You can use this in the real world:

In n*egotiations* with these people:

'Options' People

Do not follow a fixed procedure for the negotiation. Concentrate on the choices and possibilities and discuss all them

'Procedures' People

Lay out a procedure for the negotiation. Don't give them with options or choices and don't expect them to decide on alternatives.

In *managing* these people:

'Options' People

Talk about the possibilities and alternatives. Tell them to think of new ways. Do not expect them to follow routines. Make sure that they do not violate procedures.

'Procedures' People

Stress the procedures to do the work. Make sure there are procedures in place and that the person understands them. Be prepared to assist if the procedure fails.

Influencing Language

'Options' People

Alternatives, reasons, options, choices, possibilities etc.

'Procedures' People

Correct way, procedure, known way, right way, proven way etc.

CHUNK SIZE

The need for details in an individual's life throws two categories of people at us- one, the detailed or specific person, and two, those who prefer large chunks of information or the global person.

Specific people like to work with all the small details. They like to understand and go into pieces of work with the minutest of detail.

In contrast, Global people like to talk in big pictures and are not interested in details at all. They are conceptual and abstract. They'd rather give you the overall framework or brief of what is happening than go into details.

You know when someone is specific and when someone is global just by asking them any question and analyzing their response.

Specific people will give you all the details and go to great lengths to explain everything when you ask questions. Specific people become frustrated with Global People because there is no detail in what they say.

However, Global people give you an overview without details. They tend to use large generalizations. Global people become frustrated with Specific people because they go too far into detail.

Apply this to the real world:

In *negotiations* with these people:

Specific

Avoid generalizations and vagueness. Break things down into the detail and be specific. Present things in logical sequences.

Global

Avoid details and present the bigger picture.

In *managing* these people:

Specific

Tell the person in detail what needs to be done and ensure that there is a logical sequence. Do not expect them to think about the bigger picture

Global

Skip the details and give the person a broad overview. Tell them what the end game is and let them fill in the rest.

Influencing Language

Specific

Next, then, precisely, exactly, specifically, first, second, details etc.

Global

Big picture, framework, in brief, result, generally, overview etc.

CONVINCER

People make decisions and are convinced for only one of four reasons:

It looks right

    It feels right

        It sounds right

It makes sense

How do you find out what kind of person uses what reason to make a decision?

Ask them this question:

Why did you decide xyz?

What their response will tell you:

The 'Looks right' people do things because the representation that they make to themselves is a picture that literally looks right. They will use visual words when describing their decision.

The 'Feel right' people do things because the representation they make to themselves is a sensation in some part of their body which literally feels right. They use kinesthetic words when describing their decision.

'Sounds right' people do things because the representation they make to themselves is a series of words which literally sounds right to them. They will use auditory words when describing their decision.

'Makes sense' people do things because the representation they make to themselves is based on logic which in their own mind, they know, is correct. They will use auditory words when describing their decision and they will use facts, data and reason.

Utilize it in the real world:

In *negotiations* with these people:

Use the appropriate language patterns that match their decision process. If you are providing learning materials, make sure they are appropriate for the person – i.e. pictures, diagrams, facts, data etc.

In *managing* these people:

'Looks right'

Paint a picture in words, draw a diagram, and give them pictorial references to explain things to them. Let their imagination flow free. Show them how to do it.

'Feels right'

Get their internal senses working by letting them discern what they have to do. Let them get their hands on the task under supervision, and touch, feel and experience what needs to be done.

'Sounds right'

Have them describe to themselves in internal dialogue or in an appropriate tone of voice what they are supposed to do. Tell them things. Tell them what others say. They will make decisions after exploring all that they have heard.

'Makes sense'

They are the logical ones, so give them reasons for what you want them to do. Let them read instructions on how to do the job. Give them facts, statistics and data.

Influencing language

Use appropriate language, as in, what suits each type of person to help them make their decisions. (We are going to look into this in greater detail in the next chapter)

Time for some action. Here's an exercise to test what you have learnt till now.

ELICITING META-PROGRAMMES

Part 1:

Now that you have seen what makes up each of the Meta programmes, what preferences do you have?

Take time out to read through each again and write down below what your own Meta programmes are for your self-awareness and why?

- Towards/Away

- Frame of Reference

- Sameness/Difference

- Reason

- Chunk Size

- Convincer

Part 2:

The next step is that in the coming week, listen very hard to your colleagues and friends and elicit their Meta programmes.

Write these down and then formulate a strategy of how best to communicate to a few selected persons.

3 - 3

How To Communicate With Different Types Of People

Greetings! Friend...

You have reached the third part of the Effective Communication course.

In the previous chapter you learnt how to enter other people's "world" while communicating with them, so that you are at par with them and are able to work with them comfortably.

Your communication skills, in fact, have jumped a few scales above now and armed with this new talent you can nearly rule the roost!

Internal Representational Systems

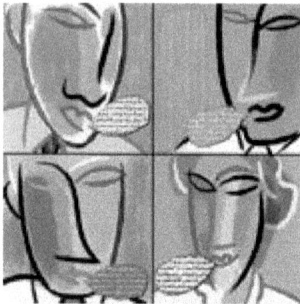

From the earlier chapters, you must already be familiar with making internal representations and Convincer, a Meta programme that describes the way people think and what they base their decisions on. We have also described that information comes in one of 5 main senses.

Well, it is now time to put all of this together by recognizing the thinking process of a person. This, we will accomplish by listening to the verbal indicators that they use in everyday speech and then using this information to design the way we communicate with them.

Remember, people like people who are like themselves!

For example, if Greg and Lily meet for the first time at a party, they will hit it off easily if both are the "It looks right" decision-making people. Since they both use mainly visual indicators they will find it easier to communicate and explain things to each other by showing real objects or by painting a diagram or by creating a picture in their minds' eye.

So, below is a list of indicators of the words that people use for the 3 main modalities:

Visual	Auditory	Kinesthetic	Unspecified
See	Hear	Fell	Sense
Look	Listen	Touch	Experience
View	Sounds	Grasp	Understand
Appear	Make music	Get hold of	Think
Show	Harmonize	Slip through	Learn
Dawn	Tune in/out	Catch on	Process
Reveal	Be all ears	Tap into	Decide
Envision	Rings a bell	Make contact	Motivate
Illuminate	Silence	Throw out	Consider
Imagine	Be heard	Turn around	Change
Clear	Resonate	Hard	Perceive
Foggy	Deaf	Unfeeling	Insensitive
Focused	Mellifluous	Concrete	Distinct
Hazy	Dissonance	Get a handle	Know
Picture	Unhearing	Solid	

Below is a list of indicator phrases that people use. Which ones do you use most often?

Visual	Auditory	Kinesthetic
An eyeful	Afterthought	All washed up
Appears to me	Blabbermouth	Boils down to
Beyond a shadow of a doubt	Call on	Chip off the old block
Birds eye view	Clear as a bell	Come to grips with
Catch a glimpse of	Clearly expressed	Control yourself
Clear cut	Describe in detail	Cool/calm/collected
Dim view	Earful	Firm foundations
Flashed on	Enquire into	Get a handle on
Get a perspective on	Give me your ear	Get a load of this
Get a scope on	Give you a call	Get in touch with
Hazy idea	Given amount of	Get the drift of
In light of	Grant an audience	Get your back up
In person	Heard voices	Hand in hand
In view of	Hidden message	Hand in there
Looks like	Hold your tongue	Heated argument
Make a scene	Ideal talk	Hold it
Mental image	Key note speaker	Hold on
Mental picture	Loud and clear	Hot head
Minds eye	Manner of speaking	Keep your shirt on
Naked eye	Pay attention to	Lay cards on the table
Paint a picture	Power of speech	Pain in the neck
See to it	State your purpose	Pull some strings
Short sighted	To tell the truth	Sharp as a tack
Showing off	Tongue-tied	Slipped my mind
Sight for sore eyes	Tuned in/tuned	Smooth operator

	out	
Staring off into space	Unheard of	So-so
Take a peak	Utterly	Start from scratch
Tunnel vision	Voiced an opinion	Stuff upper lip
Under your nose	Well informed	Stuffed shirt
Up front	Within hearing	Too much hassle
Well defined	Word for word	Topsy-turvy

YOUR REPRESENTATIONAL SYSTEM

What words do you use the most?

How do you think?

How would you best learn a new material? Through a diagram? By listening? Or by doing and feeling?

What category do you fit into the most?

Think about your friends and colleagues at work. What modalities do they use?

If you know that someone is visual – when communicating with him/her you should draw a picture or diagram and use phrases such as "Can you see it?" and "Just imagine" etc.

Eliciting thinking patterns through eye movement

Researchers, in the late seventies and early eighties, discovered that people move their eyes in a certain way when they think.

It was also noticed that students, when asked a series of questions, had structured pattern eye movements while thinking.

Researchers therefore concluded that by looking at someone's eyes, you could tell how they think.

It is true that you can tell the way people are constructing their thoughts by observing their eye movements.

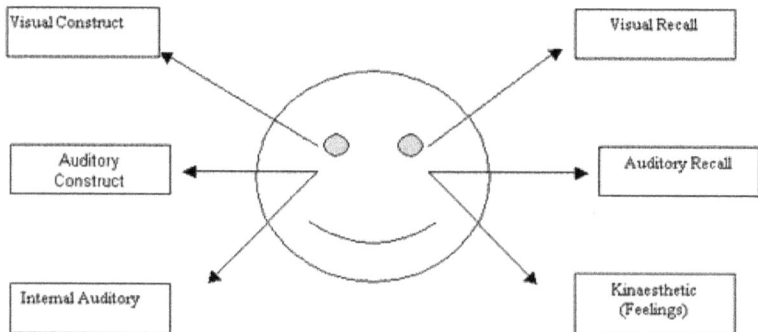

Visual Construct

Visual Recall

Auditory Construct

Auditory Recall

Internal Auditory

Kinaesthetic (Feelings)

The above picture is how a person looks when you are facing him/her.

The basic rule of eye movement pattern works this way:

Direction	Meaning
Looking up	Visualizing
Looking horizontally to left and right	Remembering or constructing sounds
Looking down to left	Accessing feelings
Looking down to right	Talking to self

Visual Recall

This is when you are recalling images from the past. You are drawing them from your memory and these are things you have seen before.

Questions to ask?

"What did your curtains look like when you were a teenager?"

"What does your car look like?"

"What was your nanny's name?"

Visual Construct

This happens when you are visualizing something you have never seen before. These are images you are making up in your head.

Sometimes you can use this one to see if people are lying to you!

Questions to ask?

"What would your car look like if it had a soft top?"

"What would your house look like if it were painted red?"

"What would you look like if you lost 3 stone in weight?"

Auditory Recall

This is when you remember sounds or voices that you have heard before or things that you have said to yourself before. These sounds are stored in your memory bank and you are actually extracting it from its location.

It's this ability that helps you recognize a voice over the phone even before the person says his/her name.

Questions to ask?

"Can you remember the sound of your grandfather's voice?"

"Can you remember what you said to yourself when you stole that pie from the oven?"

"What was the last thing I said?"

Auditory Construct

This is when you are making up sounds that you have never heard before.

Questions to ask?

"What would the national anthem sound like if it were played on the flute?"

"What would I sound like if I were fluent in Spanish?"

Kinesthetic

This involves accessing your feelings.

Questions to ask?

"What does it feel like to touch this sand paper?"

"What does it feel like to be so popular?"

Internal Auditory

This is where your eyes go when you are having internal dialogue and talking to yourself.

Questions to ask?

"Will you be able to get through this interview without getting nervous?"

"Can you recite 'Three Lions' to yourself?"

Since communication is all about rapport building, we have to be able to mirror and match another person's preferred learning and thinking style.

By observing words that people use and how they move their eyes we can understand their strategy. However, don't always look for strategies in people's eyes. This is because not all eye movements indicate one.

However, in order to communicate effectively we need to study action signals put forward by people and then modify our behavior, physiology and words so that they can easily relate to us.

After all, that is what effective communication is all about, right?

Okay, that's it for this module!

See you next time with how to build up rapport with anyone and how to put together everything you have learned so far.

3 - 4

How To Be A Great Communicator And Build Up Rapport Effortlessly

Building Rapport

You meet different types of people everyday. It is not possible to make and maintain a good relationship with all of them. No one clicks with every person he/she meets. However, it's important for you to create positive interactions with those who can push your buttons.

Communication needs to be result oriented. Building rapport is the ultimate tool for producing results and is vital for effective communication. The foundation for any meaningful interaction, it makes you more memorable and can be critical in your personal life and career.

Building rapport is similar to building a bridge over a river. The stronger the bridge, the more it can carry. In a relationship, you can ask for more if you have better rapport with the other person.

Irrespective of your knowledge about the person, there are 6 main steps to establish rapport with anyone.

Communication is much more than exchange of words. In fact, 93% of all communication is down to the tonality of your voice and your body language. So, building rapport is far more than just talking about common experiences.

However, people like people when they resemble themselves.

When they don't, it is difficult to have any kind of relationship, let

alone an effective one!

Some people easily build rapport with others. Take a look into your past. Was building rapport an easy a job for you?

Even if you are a master rapport builder, for sure you've also had times when you thought, "Oh, what am I going to do and say next?"

Everyone has such experiences.

Or consider an entirely different situation. You are so tired and have a terrible headache. Then a friend or colleague comes jumping in and full of energy, wanting to talk your head off?

There have also been times, for sure, when you turned out to be the irritating friend.

Ok, let's take a look at the 6 things you need to do to build rapport.

1. Match the persons sensory modality

People like to have relationship with those who think and behave like themselves, or even with those who have similar background. Matching and mirroring the way others think and talk is a good way to build rapport with them.

There is slight difference between mirroring and matching. Mirroring is quite similar to looking into a mirror. The time difference between the actions of both parties is negligible. However, in matching you would have to wait for your turn to repeat the action of the other party.

Take a look at the portion about visual, auditory and kinesthetic modalities. It's time for you to put it into practice.

Take note of the indicator words that the person is using and use words/phrases from the same modality. Also, look out for eye movements to spot thinking patterns.

2. Mirror the persons Physiology

Have you ever noticed that a group of teenagers who are friends bear similarities in their clothing, vocabulary and movements?

People who are in rapport have a tendency to dress in a similar way or have matching body language.

Mirroring the physiology of someone you're talking to can make him/her feel comfortable. Copying the person's posture, facial expressions, hand gestures, movements and even their eye blinking, will cause their body to say unconsciously to their mind that this person is like me!

3. Matching their voice

You should match the tone, tempo, timbre and the volume of the person's voice. If the person is slow and deliberate, he will feel comfortable if you are the same way. You should also try, when you speak, to use the keywords that they use a lot.

For examples: "Alright", "Actually", "You know what I mean"

4. Matching their breathing

If there is a big difference in the breathing pattern of two people in conversation, both of them would feel uncomfortable. If you want to build rapport with someone, you need to match the rhythm of breathing of the other person by moving your foot or finger at the same pace.

5. Matching how they deal with information

Different people deal with information differently. Some are detail oriented and some prefer it brief. You need to match the other person's way of dealing with information.

If you get this wrong you will find it very difficult to build rapport as the detailed oriented person will be yearning for more information and the other type of person will soon be yawning!

6. Matching common experiences

Suppose, you are a long way from home and met someone, who is a total stranger, and discovered he is from your own hometown. Before long, you will find yourself in a very lively conversation with the guy, looking for experiences in common.

Consider the opposite case. You are in a restaurant and everybody at your table has been served their food but you. How do you feel? Out of place?

This is all about finding some commonality. If both parties have matching experiences, interests, backgrounds, values and beliefs, they have greater chance to be in rapport.

One point to bear in mind is that you need to be subtle when you are matching and mirroring. Be careful not to exceed the limits. Typically, however, the other person will not notice it.

You can develop your ability to observe other people to such an extent that you will begin to see and even predict people's reactions to communications. This is known as calibration and is a way of determining whether you are in rapport with someone.

Increasing levels of rapport

Matching Modalities

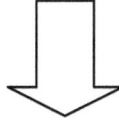

⬇

Matching the persons physiology

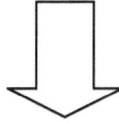

⬇

Matching their voice

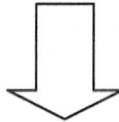

⬇

Matching their breathing patterns

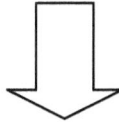

⬇

Matching how they deal with information Chunk Size

⬇

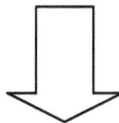

Matching common experiences

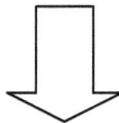

⬇

That's it for this chapter!

Don't forget to try it all out!!

How To Make Smalltalk With People

Welcome to part 5 of Effective Communication Skills!

"The gift of gab" or the ability to enter a new or unfamiliar situation and begin to engage others in conversation is a widely admired skill. Many people wrongly consider it as an innate ability that one is born with. The ability to make small talk is not a natural gift but an acquired skill.

One of the most sought-after skills, the ability to make successful small talk can be learned and perfected through practice. This skill can play a vital role in boosting your self confidence and can be critical in your personal and professional life.

For most people, starting a conversation with unfamiliar people is a difficult and painful task. They would rather pull their toe nails out than actually have to go up to someone they have never met before and strike up a conversation!

This session is all about how to communicate with people you have never met before. You can use the techniques even with people whom you find really incommunicative or in a difficult situation.

Meeting people for the first time can be a very daunting task. However, if you understand all about other people and how they like to communicate and what they like to talk about, then meeting people for the first time can be an enjoyable experience.

The main difficulty you face in starting a small talk with an unfamiliar person is that you put yourself under tremendous pressure to talk. You will start asking yourself questions like:

What should **I** talk about?

What shall **I** say?

How will **I** fill this silence in the conversation?

You are very concerned about how others are evaluating you while you are making small talk. You are concerned not only for the evaluation during the talk but also for the judgment that goes beyond the conversation. You are too busy thinking of what to say that you forget about communicating with the other person!

BECOME AN EXPERT LISTENER

"You say it best when you say nothing at all"

Boyzone

The best conversationalists in this world are the best listeners. You must resist the urge to dominate the conversation. In fact, the person who says the least is often the best communicator. Then why should you be racking your brains thinking of things to say every time?

In a conversation, you are listening means the other person is talking. Becoming an expert listener makes you a good conversationalist. During the conversation lean slightly forward, face the other person directly, and don't miss a single word. Most people are poor listeners because they are busy preparing a reply while the other person is still speaking.

When you go into a situation where you are meeting someone for the first time, you need to be very much focused on him/her. You must treat that person as if he/she is the most important person in the world. Ask questions that evoke interest in them and be intrigued about them.

Small talks depend very much on your ability to ask questions and to listen attentively to the answers. Wait for your turn to speak. The others person will ask about you at any point during the conversation. Don't talk for too long. Always try to ask open-ended questions.

So, how can you start and hold a good conversation?

To do this, it is important to understand what other people like to talk about.

Here is the TOP 5 in order:

1. THEMSELVES!

You know how much you love to talk about how you dribbled the ball and beat three defenders in a row yesterday or about your high grades in the last exam.

Yes, people love to talk about themselves.

The best way to build rapport with someone and to hold a conversation is letting them to talk about their favorite subject - THEMSELVES!

Always ask for their opinion, their stand and more importantly about their achievements.

Suppose you are the representative of a magazine and you want to get the opinion of a business person. How will you start the conversation if you ran into him one day?

Normally you will start like, "Hello, my name is..." Once you reveal your identity the person will try to keep away from you.

What if you start the conversation like, "Hello Mr. Jobs. So you made it to the BOD of Avalon Inc?" Mr. Jobs will surely have something to say about it.

Ask question to get them to talk about themselves and then ask some more questions, and then some more!

He or she will love you for it!

2. THEIR OWN OPINIONS

An opinion is something everyone has got. And people love to air their one on anything and everything.

"What do you think of the way Manchester United has played this year?"
"What is your opinion on the strike?"
"What do you think of XYZ programme?"

Ask these questions, you will have your new friend talking for hours!

Be careful not to be argumentative even if your opinion differs. However, if you want to conclude, you can make a sharp exit by refuting his opinion.

3. OTHER PEOPLE

Who doesn't want to gossip?

People love to talk about other people. You can easily start a conversation by talking about someone the other party has an interest in.

"Heard your niece is the new Ms California. Is she planning for a career in modeling?"

You will get everything from how much the niece loves the person to her appointments till 2050.

4. THINGS

"I love YOUR car, what model is it?"

All are proud of their possessions and never spoil a chance to talk about them. You will surely get a detailed description of the vehicle for the above question.

You can also start an interesting conversation by mentioning about anything that can evoke an interest in the other party. You know how long two teenage boys can talk about girls.

5. YOU!

So you have reached the bottom of the list. It's quite unfortunate that the last thing people want to talk about is YOU!

As you are trying to keep the conversation focused on the other person, you will have to wait for your turn to speak about yourself. And worse, you cannot talk about what you want to. Whatever you say should be connected to what the other person has already said.

Following is an action plan to start and hold a conversation. Try it out next time.

ACTION PLAN

- **You don't have to think munch or worry about what to say. Just have an idea of the other person and go ahead.**
- **Carefully listen and ask relevant questions about the other person.**
- **Then you can take some liberty and ask some more questions!**
- **Always think about "YOU" instead of "I."**
- **Find the other person's favorite 5 subjects and talk about them in order!**
- **Don't talk about yourself until the other person asks.**
- **Have a lot of fun!**

Making the first move

You are in a party and whenever that tall girl with brown hair smiles your heart skips a beat. You want to make the first move, but you don't have the courage.

Your brain is in search of the hundred reasons why the girl will not like you. You are sure that you will be rejected because there are better men. And worse, you have nothing to say to the girl. Simply you are scared.

Not an unfamiliar situation, right?

What if the girl is thinking exactly the same thing?

Never spoil a chance to make the first move. You don't have to worry about or be scared of a possible rejection. Take a deep breath, go to the person and ask an opening question.

When you meet a person at a particular place you can be sure of one thing. Some common interests brought both of you there. And you know how to start and hold a conversation with someone who shares some interests with you.

Small talk is the foundation of any serious conversation. So it's always good to start off with small talk. Start on simple topics of conversation and then move on.

**"There are no uninteresting people,
only disinterested listeners!"**

Okay! That's it for this module!

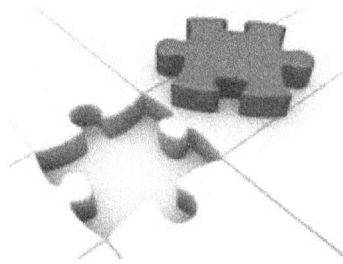

3 - 6

Giving And Receiving Feedback

Welcome to the final part of the communications course, I hope you have enjoyed it.

This chapter is all about giving and receiving feedback.

Giving feedback

Feedback is a powerful communication tool. It can help people know their behavior and find out things about themselves that they might not have considered. The ability to give and solicit feedback makes you a good communicator.

Giving feedback is one of the most difficult things in communication. Some people struggle with giving proper feedback in their personal and professional lives. Without knowing how to give feedback, it can be uncomfortable and unpleasant for both the giver and the receiver.

A feedback should be given in a way that the receiver can use it to either make improvements or keep up the good work. This communication tool is widely used in education and is essential for learning and continuous improvement. Constructive feedbacks motivate people.

A corrective feedback is supposed to relay specific information that provides the recipient guidance and direction in an activity. Many people find it difficult to give corrective feedback. However, it is possible to learn techniques for effectively offering both praise and correction.

Giving feedback is an integral part of the coaching process that provides your staff members with support and direction, and ultimately results in increased participation. Both positive and negative feedbacks have their part to play. It is the best way to convey your staff what you think about a particular work or performance.

Principles of feedback

Following are the seven principles of feedback.

1. Choose correct timing for feedback

Feedback is most helpful and effective when given at the earliest opportunity after the given behavior or incident has occurred. Immediate feedback will help to reinforce a correct behavior and make it more likely to happen again.

Corrective feedback also is the most effective when given as soon as possible. If a wrong behavior is not corrected with corrective feedback at the earliest possible moment, the staff member may repeat it and set a bad precedence. However, in the case of corrective feedback, the receiver's willingness to hear it is very important.

2. Ask for self assessment

In a communication process, the willingness of the receiver to hear the feedback is very important. To ensure the participation of the other party, the sender needs to create an open atmosphere before giving a corrective feedback.

Asking the person for self-assessment may help involve him/her in the feedback process. It can create an open atmosphere and promote dialogue between the sender and the receiver. In fact, few people are not aware of the gravity of the mistakes they have committed or the job they have done well.

Allowing the person to voice his/her opinions before providing your own assessment of performance can lead to more positive results. Such opportunities for self assessment may help the person to gradually assume more responsibility without supervision.

3. Focus on specifics

"I liked the way you trained your subordinate. You outlined the procedure in writing and then listened as he relayed back to you the process. Great job!"

Take a look at the above statement.

Feedbacks should not be linked to the personality or character of the person. You should focus on a specific correct or incorrect behavior. Such feedbacks can make the person more willing and able to change. A feedback should be specific, visible and measurable in order to be effective.

For example, when providing corrective feedback:

Do: "When you were talking to customer xyz, I noticed that you forgot to use her name"

Don't: "You are not building rapport with the customer"

When providing praise:

Do: "When you spoke to customer xyz, I noticed that you used really good open and closed questioning techniques"

Don't: "You communicated well there"

4. Limit feedback to a few important points

A feedback should address the needs of you and the other person. However, it should be limited to a few very important points.

Good coaches and communicators identify one or two critical areas and help the person address them one at a time. Examination of many aspects of behavior at one time is too hard to be effective.

Restrict your feedback to one or two important points so that you do not overwhelm the other person with too many things to consider.

5. Provide more praise than corrective feedback

Praise is usually given for exemplary work or behavior that exceeds expectations. However, positive reinforcement can always play an important role in bringing about change. The sad thing is that people always focus on negatives.

When you give corrective feedback, remember to point out correct behaviors first. This is as important as pointing out mistakes and areas that need improvement. And always try to conclude the conversation in a positive manner.

6. Give praise for expected performance

Sometimes a positive appraisal or a word of praise can make miracles. Praise is a strong motivator and nothing is more encouraging than acceptance.

People deserve to be praised for doing their job to the expected level. In fact, positive feedbacks are enjoyable for both the sender and the receiver.

One thing you have to keep in mind is that praising anyone who meets established standards is as important as praising the exceptional performer.

Tell the person exactly why you are praising him/her in clear and specific words.

Remember, praise may be what it takes to turn an average employee into an exceptional one.

7. Develop Action Plans

Effective implementation of any process needs an action plan. You need to work together with subordinates to identify the desired performance or result and how it can be achieved. Also decide a deadline for the completion of the steps.

Useful techniques to use when giving feedback

Following are some useful techniques you can use in feedback sessions:

Open-ended Questioning	Reflecting Back	Maintaining Silence

Active Listening	Initiating action & Offering ideas

Gaining Ownership	Summarizing	Being Sensitive

Open-ended questioning

Open-ended questions do not have a preset limit. They promote continued conversation and allow the person to give more details. They are meant to draw out more information and often give more insight into the other person's feelings.

Consider the following question.

"Do you like the new program?"

The question can be answered with a yes or no, or with a simple statement of fact.

What about asking the following question instead?

"What are your concerns about this new program?"

Use words like:

What?

How?

Who?

Tell me?

Avoid closed questions when you are trying to get more information from someone.

Avoid words like:

Do you?

Did you?

Have you?

Also be careful with the use of the word "Why," especially when you are giving feedback. The person may think that you are blaming him/her or being critical if you use it.

Reflecting Back

You can use the other person's complaints as a tool to create an open atmosphere. This is about putting what the other person has said into your own words and reflecting it back. This technique is known as paraphrasing.

Paraphrasing is a good way to show that you are listening and more importantly that you are listening and understanding!

For example:

The other person – "I always seem to get the rough end of the stick - no-one listens to me at all……."

You – "You seem concerned that no-one listens to you and that you seem to be getting a dumb deal"

Maintaining Silence

You can convey a lot of things via silence. Moreover, you can encourage the person to take his/her time and give an appropriate reply. Always give the other person time to think through their reply.

Silence is not an opportunity to feel uncomfortable or lose your interest in the conversation. Be careful to maintain eye contact and demonstrate an interest.

Summarizing

The other person needs to be convinced that you have heard everything correctly and understood from his/her perspective. Summarize the output of the meeting and action plan and recite it to him/her.

Then you can conclude the discussion and focus on planning for the future.

Example: "The three major issues you raised were......"

"To summarize then......"

Being Sensitive

A good communicator is an empathetic person. Being sensitive to the needs of the person is important as they may reject the feedback initially. Give the person space and time to think. This may help him/her to absorb the feedback in its true sense.

Initiating Action and Offering Ideas

Feedback is always associated with improvement. So giving a well-structured action plan and some ideas for the betterment of the performance can be very constructive.

Consider the following example.

"Can you think of an action that would help build on your skills in this area?"

Do not allow your personal opinion to reflect in the ideas you offer. You have many other opportunities to do that.

Gaining Ownership

You need to make the person feel comfortable to act in line with your feedback. For this, you can help him/her to integrate the feedback into his/her experience. Then he/she can have a point of view other than yours.

Linking the feedback as much as possible to business results and objectives will help increase ownership. Remember, any change in behaviour will only occur through acceptance and ownership of the feedback by that person.

Receiving Feedback

There are times when you face the other side of the coin too. While giving feedback, remember that some time or the other you will also be at, let's just call it the 'receiving end'. So be prepared.

Etch this onto your mind- As long as the feedback comes to you in a non-judgmental and appropriate fashion accept it is as a valuable piece of information for learning and for our continued development as a person.

This valuable piece of 'information' is what we call constructive feedback and it is critical for self-development and growth.

Here are some points to remember when you receive feedback:

Don't shy away from constructive feedback, welcome it

- Accept feedback of any sort for what it is – information
- Evaluate the feedback before responding
- Make your own choice about what you intend to do with the information

The feedback emotional rollercoaster

Here's a feedback model that you should keep in mind while giving or receiving feedback.

D A W A

DENIAL

This is typically associated with jumping the gun. Most people while receiving feedback tend to jump at it and immediately get defensiveness by arguing, denying or justifying. Try to avoid it. This just gets in the way of appreciation of the information you are being given.

ANGER

So you've been told that your work is not as good as what it ought to be. Here comes Anger! Coming right after denial where you said, "It's as good as always", you get angry as the feedback stews in your mind and body. The immediate reaction is to fume!

WITHDRAWAL

Once the anger dies down, people get time to reflect and ponder on the feedback. "Well, I have been making more mistakes then normal" This is when time is taken out to mull over the feedback and think about what it actually means.

ACCEPTANCE

The withdrawal stage is closely followed by the final part of this model – accepting the feedback, assessing its value and the consequences of ignoring it, or using it. "I HAVE been making mistakes."

That's it for this module and the course!

Trust you have enjoyed it!

Don't forget to try out the tips.

About the Author

Mawgen is a Presenter/Trainer and delivers 1 day, 6 day, 12 ay and 30 day certifications in behavioural psychology and NLP to individuals and corporate companies. He also works 1-on-1 with clients doing coaching and personal breakthrough sessions using techniques he received from his world class training and years of experience.

Currently he is the principal trainer and head of research for Mawgen Schoeman Training & Events and VUE NLP Training Co.

Mawgen delivers his courses in a very down to earth and easy to understand manner. Nothing that's needed is taken out and no extra jargon that's not needed is put in.

As Mawgen would put it 'It's about getting results at the end of every session or training while enjoying the process of discovery that matters. It's about creating excellence while staying true to yourself without being destructive to the people and environment around you.'

His outlook will help you be the best you can be, as he's done over the years with others.

Credentials...

While studying Microbiology at the University of South South Africa, Mawgen started his personal development journey in South Africa by studying with local training institutes and assisting on training seminars. He then moved to the United Kingdom where he started his international training journey.

Mawgen is certified through the IAH (International Association of Hypnonis) as a Hypnoanalyst and started his coaching business by assisting clients create change in their lives.

He then moved on to complete his NLP Practitioner and Master Practitioner certifications through the ABNLP and started delivering workshops to corporate companies as an addition to the coaching business.

Mawgen travelled to Sydney, Australia to received his NLP Trainers Training certification (ABNLP Certified) as well as the Time Line Therapy® Trainers) and Creating Your Future® Master Coaching (ABNLP Certified) Certifications.

The year after Mawgen also received the Master Time Line Therapy® techniques (TLTA Certified certification.

While delivering internationally certified NLP Practitioner and Master Practitioner certifications, Seminars for Corporate companies in the United Kingdom and South Africa, and seeing clients on a 1-on-1 basis, Mawgen is the head of research and principal trainer in VUE NLP and coaching techniques.

He also teaches individuals how to become magical speakers, presenters and trainers by sharing his knowledge from world class courses and vast experience he's picked up over the last 12 years.

Credentials in a nutshell:

Successful Author

Corporate Presenter/Trainer

ABNLP Certified Practitioner, Master Practitioner and Trainer

IAH Certified Hypnoanalyst

ABH Certified Master Hypnotherapist

Creator and Master Trainer of VUE NLP and VUE Life Coaching Techniques
Principal trainer for MS Training And Events and also for VUE NLP And Coaching Co.

Why study with www.nlpmindsolutions.com?

First of all, our beliefs that govern how we create our products, how we deliver our seminars, how we support you during and after courses and 1-on-1 sessions, how we define ourselves in the market, and how we insure you receive the highest quality available:

1. If our clients are successful, we are successful. We understand how important your journey is during your training and we don't stop there. It's equally important whether YOU achieve results from spending time with us and not just us as a training provider. When you join us on the presenter/trainer courses, we make sure you become a successful presenter trainer. When you join us on the NLP and personal development certifications, we make sure YOU achieve results in your personal life.

2. Focus on quality, not quantity. We have a Trainer to delegate ratio. This means that you always receive feedback and personal tutoring from a certified trainer. We made sure we didn't learn from assistant when we did our training and we'll make sure you never have to either.

3. We teach you content of what we already are successful in. The things we aren't we don't' teach. We would rather refer you to specialists that are successful in what you are interested in. You can be sure that what we do present, we've learned and mastered through experience.

You can contact Mawgen Schoeman at
mawgen@nlpmindsolutions.com

www.ingramcontent.com/pod-product-compliance
Lightning Source LLC
Chambersburg PA
CBHW051959090426
42741CB00008B/1469